AI

AND

THE FUTURE OF SMART MARKETING

THE GAME CHANGER FOR THE MODERN BUSINESS

TAMIL SELVI K GANESAN

notionpress.com

INDIA • SINGAPORE • MALAYSIA

ISBN 979-8-89588-337-2

CONTENTS

CONTENTS

Chapter 1
The AI Marketing Revolution

"Marketing is everywhere". From the first time someone traded one thing for another, to the ads we scroll past on our phones today, it's all marketing. It's about getting the right products to the right people at the right time and making sure they know why it's right for them. For a long time, figuring out the best way to do this was mostly guesswork and gut feeling. Then, AI came into the picture.

What is AI? Think of it as a smart helper that's good at looking at information and making sense of it. It can learn from what it sees, make decisions based on that learning, and even improve how it makes those decisions over time. In marketing, AI can do things like find the best places and times to show ads, create messages that speak directly to what people want, and talk to customers on websites to help them find what they need.

AI in marketing is a big deal because it changes how we do things. It's not just a small step forward; it's a whole new way of connecting with people. Marketing has always been there, but AI lets us understand and reach out to people in ways we couldn't before.

Definition and Importance of AI in Marketing

What is AI in Marketing?

AI in marketing is the technology that helps us understand and connect with customers in effective ways. AI's impact on marketing is notable for its real-time analysis of vast data. Many well-known companies have effectively used AI in their marketing strategies. It involves using computers to analyze data, predict customer behavior, and automate communication. This isn't about making guesses; it's about using real data and intelligent algorithms to inform decisions. As a result, AI marketing tools become increasingly accurate in performing tasks and improving marketing solutions.

Why is it Important?

Understanding Customers: AI allows us to dive deep into customer data. This helps in understanding patterns like shopping behaviors, preferences, and trends. For example, Netflix uses AI to suggest shows and movies by analyzing your watching habits.

Efficiency: Automating tasks with AI, such as sending emails or posting on social media, saves a considerable amount of time and money. Persado, a marketing language platform, uses AI to create engaging content quickly, something that would take much longer for a person to accomplish.

Personalisation: Personalised marketing is more effective. AI helps tailor marketing messages for individual customers, making them feel understood and valued. Starbucks, for example, uses AI in its app to give you recommendations and discounts that match your preferences.

Predictive Analysis: AI doesn't predict the future in the way fortune tellers do, but it can make educated guesses based on data trends. This helps companies anticipate market demands and customer needs, staying ahead in their industry.

AI in marketing is essentially about leveraging technology to enhance our understanding of customers, streamline marketing operations, offer personalised experiences, and predict future trends. It's about making marketing not just more efficient, but also more relevant and responsive to the needs and desires of customers.

Evolution of AI in Marketing Practices

The journey of AI in marketing is, how technology has grown from simple tools to complex systems that can think and learn almost like a human. This evolution has changed marketing from broad strategies aimed at everyone to tailored approaches designed for each individual.

At the Start

Marketing used to be about getting a message out to as many people as possible, like ads on billboards or TV. Back then, computers helped a little, mainly to keep track of sales or customer information.

When the Internet Changed Everything

Once everyone started using the internet, marketing began to change. Websites and emails made it easier to talk directly to customers. Collecting information got easier too, so marketers began to understand what people liked and didn't like customer needs and wants. This was important for AI because AI needs much information to learn and improve.

AI Steps In

With AI, things really started to change. Now, it wasn't just about collecting information but also understanding it quickly and in big amounts. This brought us things like emails that send themselves when you're most likely to open them, chatbots that answer questions any time of the day, and websites that show you stuff you're actually interested in.

AI Now

Today, AI is like a team member in marketing. It helps write ads, decides the best time and place to show them, and even helps figure out what new products people might like. It's all about making sure the marketing fits you specifically, not just anyone.

Looking Ahead

In the future, AI is going to be even smarter and more a part of our daily experiences. Think about talking to a virtual assistant who knows exactly what you need before you ask, or trying on clothes in a digital store that feels almost real. AI is going to make everything more about you than ever.

Importance and Relevance of AI in the Modern Marketing Landscape

AI has become a regular part of our daily lives, shaping the way we do everyday tasks without us even noticing most of the time. It helps us by suggesting what to buy next when we're shopping online, finding the fastest route on our commutes, and even deciding what we might want to watch next. It's like having a helpful assistant who knows our preferences and makes our daily lives a bit easier. AI is everywhere, making our interactions smoother and our decisions quicker.

As we look into the importance and relevance of AI in the modern marketing landscape for 2024, it's clear that AI is no longer just an auxiliary tool; it's becoming central to how brands engage with consumers and manage marketing processes effectively.

- **Personalization at Scale:** AI's capability to analyze extensive data allows businesses to offer highly personalized customer experiences. For instance, AI can manage individualized marketing at a scale that was previously unmanageable, adjusting content dynamically to match user preferences and behaviors. This level of personalization not only enhances the customer experience but significantly boosts engagement and conversion rates.

- **Efficiency and Automation:** AI streamlines numerous routine tasks, from content generation to customer service, allowing marketing teams to focus on more strategic and creative endeavors. This shift not only improves operational efficiency but also speeds up decision-making and reduces overhead costs.

- **Advanced Analytics and Decision Making:** With AI, marketers gain deeper insights into consumer behaviors and market trends, which facilitates more informed decision-making. Predictive analytics, a subset of AI, plays a crucial role here by forecasting future trends and customer responses, thus enabling companies to craft proactive strategies that align closely with consumer expectations.

- **Content Creation and Management:** AI tools are also revolutionizing content creation by generating compelling marketing copy, videos, and images that resonate with targeted audiences. Furthermore, AI's role in content management helps ensure that the right content reaches the right audience at the optimal time, thereby maximizing the impact of marketing campaigns.

- **Challenges and Adaptation:** While the benefits are significant, integrating AI into marketing strategies comes with challenges such as ensuring the AI-generated content aligns with brand values, adapting to new technologies, and managing data privacy concerns. Overcoming these challenges requires a strategic approach and ongoing adaptation to harness AI's full potential effectively.

AI continues to evolve, and its integration into marketing becomes increasingly critical for businesses aiming to remain competitive in a digital-first world. Marketers must stay informed about the latest AI advancements and consider how these technologies can be incorporated into their marketing strategies to enhance efficiency, personalisation, and overall business growth.

How AI is reshaping marketing with real-world examples from big brands.

Netflix Masters Personalisation

Netflix is a pioneer in using AI to recommend shows and movies based on what you've watched before. This isn't just smart; it's crucial for keeping viewers hooked and subscribing month after month. The system looks at your past choices, combines this with data from millions of others, and predicts what you might like next. The result? About 80% of what people watch on Netflix comes from these recommendations. This focus on personalization keeps customer turnover low and savings high—Netflix believes this technology saves them over a billion dollars annually.

Sephora and the Beauty of AI

Sephora brings AI into play with its Virtual Artist chatbot. It uses facial recognition so you can test makeup virtually. You can try new eyeshadows or lip colors without actually using the products. This feature boosts customers' trust in what they buy and has led to a big sales boost. Also, the chatbot gives instant advice, making it easier for shoppers to find products and reducing the load on human staff.

Starbucks Gets Predictive

Starbucks uses artificial intelligence to send marketing messages that are tailored to you based on what you usually order. If you always get the same coffee, Starbucks' AI will pick up on that and might offer you a discount on your favorite drink or recommend new items you might like. This makes customers feel like Starbucks gets them and appreciates them, which makes them visit more often and spend more.

Coca-Cola Optimizes with AI

Coca-Cola uses AI to analyse sales data and decide which products to promote and where. This method helps them tailor their marketing to various groups and local tastes, boosting marketing efficiency by 30%. It's not just about selling more; it's about selling smarter, leading to improved outcomes with less waste.

Unilever's Social Media Savvy

Unilever uses AI to improve its social media ads. By studying past campaigns, AI assists Unilever in creating messages that connect well with various audiences, boosting user engagement and increasing sales. Certain campaigns have experienced a 50% rise in engagement, showing how AI can change how brands interact with customers.

Ethical Considerations

As AI becomes increasingly integral to marketing strategies, it raises several ethical considerations that businesses must navigate carefully. The most pressing issues often revolve around privacy concerns and the transparency of AI-driven decisions.

Understanding Privacy Concerns in AI-Driven Marketing

AI tech can gather, study, and save loads of personal info—like what you browse online or what you like to buy. This helps marketers fine-tune their ads really precisely, but it also brings up big worries about privacy. People are noticing more and more how their info is used and are really worried about privacy slip-ups and sharing data without permission.

Compliance with Data Protection Regulations

In response to these concerns, regions around the world have implemented stringent data protection regulations. For example:

General Data Protection Regulation (GDPR) in Europe: This regulation is one of the strictest in the world and applies to all companies operating within the EU and the EEA. It gives consumers the right to access the data collected about them, the right to have incorrect data corrected, the right to have their data erased, and more importantly, the right to have a say in the processing of their personal data.

California Consumer Privacy Act (CCPA) in the United States: This state-specific law grants California residents increased rights over their data, including the right to know what personal information is being collected and for what purpose, the right to opt out of the sale of personal information, and the right to access their personal information.

Ethical Data Usage Practices

Beyond legal compliance, companies need to adopt ethical data usage practices that respect consumer privacy. This involves:

- **Transparency is important:** Tell customers what data is collected and how it's used. This builds trust and eases worries about data use.

- **Get consent:** Ask users clearly before collecting their data. They should know and agree willingly, without any tricky tactics.

- **Data Minimization:** Only gather data needed for marketing. Don't collect tons of data just in case you might need it later.

- **Security:** Put strong security measures in place to keep your personal info safe from unauthorized access. Regularly check and update security rules to protect your details.

- **Accountability:** Make sure there are rules inside the company to make us responsible for following the law and doing the right thing. Teach employees how to protect data and have clear steps for dealing with data problems.

Bias and Fairness

AI systems in marketing depend on data to decide things. But, if the data used to teach these AI systems is unfair, then the decisions they make will probably be unfair too. This can mean targeting some groups unfairly or even leaving out possible customers because of wrong ideas in the computer programs.

If an AI system is taught mostly using data from one group of people, its suggestions and choices might not work well for others. This can cause marketing plans that unknowingly help one group more than others, which could lead to unfair treatment and missed chances.

Marketers need to keep an eye on their AI systems. They should update the data the AI uses regularly to make sure it represents all types of customers. It's important to check for any biases in the AI decisions and fix them if found.

Being clear about how AI makes decisions matters. People and regulators want to know why automated decisions are made, especially if they affect what consumers can do. By explaining how AI works and making sure it's fair, companies can earn trust and follow rules like GDPR, which asks for explanations of automatic decisions in certain situations.

Why Human Oversight Matters

Even as AI systems become more capable and autonomous, the role of human oversight in these technologies cannot be understated. This oversight is crucial not just for ensuring that AI operations are effective but also for making sure they adhere to ethical standards and reflect the core values of the company.

Human oversight serves as a critical check on the capabilities of AI systems. AI, no matter how advanced, still lacks the human capacity for judgment that considers ethical nuances and complex social contexts. Humans can see the bigger picture—a skill AI has yet to fully replicate.

Implementing Effective Human Oversight

Continuous Involvement: Humans must be involved from the onset of AI development through to its deployment and daily operation. This ongoing involvement ensures that AI decisions are continually aligned with ethical considerations and company objectives.

Decision-Making Power: While AI can process data and make recommendations, the final decisions should often rest with a human, especially in high-stakes situations. This ensures that decisions can be justified and are made with a level of empathy and understanding that AI cannot provide.

Training and Knowledge: For human oversight to be effective, those in charge of overseeing AI systems must be well-trained in both the technology and its ethical implications. Understanding how AI works, what its limitations are, and how it can potentially bias its outputs is crucial.

Regular Evaluations: AI systems should be regularly evaluated by human overseers to ensure they are performing as intended and not deviating from their programmed boundaries. This includes checking for biases that the AI might have learned as it operates.

Creating Accountability: By involving humans in the oversight of AI, companies create a system of accountability. If an AI system fails or acts in an undesirable way, it is clear who is responsible for correcting these issues.

Benefits of Human Oversight

Incorporating human oversight doesn't just mitigate risks; it also enhances the capabilities of AI systems. With humans in the loop, AI can be adjusted and fine-tuned to better meet the needs of the business and its customers. It also builds public and consumer trust in the technology, as stakeholders know that the AI's decisions are being monitored and managed responsibly.

Conclusion

AI in marketing is like having a super smart tool that knows exactly what customers want, even before they do. It looks at tons of information—from what people browse online to what they buy—and uses this to make smart guesses about what they'll want next. This makes marketing not just faster, but a lot more personal.

Chatbots powered by AI can talk to customers any time of the day, giving quick answers to questions and helping solve problems right away. This makes customers happy because they get instant help without having to wait.

AI also helps in making ads that are spot-on. It can figure out who will be most interested in what you're selling and then place ads where these people are most likely to see them. This means businesses spend less money on ads that don't work and more on ones that do.

AI is great at making sense of all the data that businesses collect. It can spot trends and patterns that tell marketers what's working and what's not. This helps them plan better campaigns that are more likely to succeed.

AI doesn't just keep things running smoothly; it also keeps getting smarter. It learns from past campaigns and improves over time, which means the more you use it, the better it gets at understanding and reaching customers.

As the world becomes more connected and digital, using AI in marketing isn't just helpful; it's essential. It allows businesses to stay relevant, understand their customers better, and create marketing strategies that hit the mark. Accepting AI in marketing means being ready for the future today, making sure your business stays ahead in a fast-moving world.

Chapter 2
Core AI Technologies in Marketing

Siri: Hey Alexa, it seems like AI is everywhere in marketing these days, doesn't it?

Alexa: It really does, Siri. It's incredible to see how AI is behind so many things we interact with daily. It's almost like a behind-the-scenes wizard, isn't it?

Siri: Exactly! It's like every time you see a digital ad perfectly tailored to your interests, AI is working its magic in the background.

Alexa: And it's not just ads! From predicting what you want to buy next to understanding how you feel about a product, AI technologies are deeply involved.

Siri: That's the beauty of it. AI isn't just a tool; it's becoming a core part of the marketing strategies. It learns from patterns and behaviors to make everything more seamless and personalized for consumers.

Alexa: And think about the speed! AI can process information and make decisions faster than any human marketing team could. It means companies can react in real-time to how their customers are interacting with their brand.

Siri: Right, the responsiveness that AI allows is something else! Plus, it's not just about being fast. It's about being precise. That's something AI excels at.

Alexa: True. It can sift through massive amounts of data to find exactly what's relevant, making sure that businesses aren't just throwing out random content.

Siri: It's like having a super-powered marketing assistant who knows precisely what to do and when to do it.

Alexa: Absolutely, Siri. And as we look ahead, it's clear that AI is not just a passing trend—it's a fundamental part of how brands will interact with us as consumers.

Siri: Couldn't agree more, Alexa. The future of marketing is here, and it's powered by AI. Let's see how this journey unfolds!

What is Deep Learning?

Deep learning, a subset of artificial intelligence, is a powerful tool that mimics the way the human brain processes information to recognize patterns and make decisions. This technology allows computers to perform complex tasks that typically require human intelligence, such as identifying objects in images or understanding spoken words.

At its core, deep learning uses a structure called a neural network, which is inspired by the neural pathways of the human brain. These networks consist of layers of nodes, or "neurons," each of which processes various aspects of the data it receives. The first layer might handle basic features, while deeper layers combine these initial features to recognize more complex patterns.

One of the most significant advantages of deep learning is its ability to learn and improve on its own. As it processes more data, a deep learning model adjusts and refines its internal parameters to minimize errors. This process, known as training, involves feeding large amounts of labeled data (data with known answers) into the neural network and gradually improving the model based on its performance.

Applications of Deep Learning in Marketing

Customer Behavior Analysis: Deep learning can analyze customer behavior patterns to predict future actions, such as the likelihood of a purchase based on browsing history or previous purchases. This allows marketers to create more targeted campaigns that are likely to convert.

Image and Voice Recognition: These technologies are used in creating more interactive and accessible customer service tools, such as voice-activated assistants and image-based search tools, enhancing the user experience on digital platforms.

Personalization: By understanding individual preferences and behaviors, deep learning enables highly personalized marketing, from customized emails to tailored website experiences, significantly enhancing customer engagement and satisfaction.

Real-Time Decision Making: Deep learning facilitates real-time analysis and decision-making, allowing businesses to adjust their strategies promptly based on immediate customer interactions and feedback. This agility is crucial in dynamic market environments.

Moreover, deep learning can optimize marketing strategies by predicting outcomes based on historical data. For instance, it can forecast the success of a marketing campaign, suggest the best times to post on social media, or even identify the most effective promotional offers for different customer segments.

As technology continues to advance, the capabilities of deep learning in marketing are only expected to grow, making it an indispensable tool for marketers aiming to leverage data-driven insights to gain a competitive edge. This technology's ability to process and learn from data at scale offers unprecedented opportunities to enhance personalization, efficiency, and effectiveness in marketing efforts.

Understanding Machine Learning

Machine learning, a core component of artificial intelligence, leverages algorithms to sift through data, learn from it, and make informed decisions. Unlike traditional software that follows explicit instructions from programmers, machine learning uses data to train models, enabling them to make predictions and decisions autonomously.

The essence of machine learning lies in its ability to process large volumes of data, extract patterns, and learn from them without human intervention. This process involves three main steps: training, validation, and testing. During training, the model is exposed to a large dataset, learning to recognize patterns and relationships within the data. In the validation phase, the model's accuracy is fine-tuned, and finally, testing evaluates its performance on unseen data.

How Machine Learning Operates in Marketing

In the context of marketing, machine learning can be applied in numerous impactful ways:

- **Customer Segmentation:** Machine learning algorithms can sift through massive datasets to identify distinct groups within a customer base. By recognizing patterns that differentiate these groups, marketers can tailor their strategies to target each segment with personalized messages and offers.

- **Recommendation Systems:** Perhaps the most familiar use of machine learning in marketing is in recommendation systems. Platforms like Amazon and Netflix use machine learning to analyze your past behavior and the behavior of others to recommend products or content you might like. This not only enhances user experience but also increases the likelihood of additional sales.

- **Predictive Analytics:** Machine learning excels in predictive analytics, where it forecasts future buyer behaviors based on historical data. This can involve predicting which leads are most likely to convert into customers, which products will see a surge in demand, or even when a customer might be at risk of churning.

- **Ad Targeting and Optimization:** Machine learning algorithms analyze numerous variables in real time to determine the best audience for a particular advertisement. They also continuously optimize campaigns, adjusting bidding strategies and ad placements to maximize return on investment.

Challenges and Considerations

While machine learning offers extensive capabilities, it also presents challenges, particularly in data quality and algorithmic bias. The quality of outputs from machine learning models is directly tied to the quality of the input data. Poor, incomplete, or biased data can lead to inaccurate predictions and discriminatory outcomes. Marketers must ensure that the data used is not only extensive and well-rounded but also representative and fair.

Furthermore, as machine learning models can be complex, understanding and interpreting the decisions made by these models can be challenging. This "black box" issue is significant in marketing, where understanding the rationale behind certain decisions, such as why a particular customer segment was targeted or not, is crucial.

As businesses continue to navigate vast amounts of data, machine learning remains an invaluable tool, providing the insights and automation necessary to drive marketing success. Its ability to learn and adapt makes it particularly effective in an environment where consumer preferences and market dynamics are constantly evolving.

Natural Language Processing (NLP)

Natural Language Processing (NLP) is a branch of artificial intelligence that bridges the gap between human communication and computer understanding. It allows machines to interpret, understand, and respond to human language in a way that is both meaningful and useful.

The core functionality of NLP involves several key processes:

- **Text Analysis:** NLP systems analyze text to understand grammar, context, and the meaning of words. This involves breaking down sentences into words and phrases and understanding the relationships between them.

- **Semantic Analysis:** This process involves deciphering the meanings and intentions behind the words. Semantic analysis helps the system understand the context in which terms are used, distinguishing between multiple meanings of a single word based on its usage.

- **Machine Translation:** NLP enables the translation of text from one language to another. This is essential for global businesses and services that cater to a diverse user base.

- **Speech Recognition:** NLP is also crucial in developing systems that can understand spoken language, converting speech into text that computers can process.

- **Chatbots and Virtual Assistants:** Using NLP, chatbots and virtual assistants such as Siri, Alexa, and Google Assistant can interact with users naturally and conversationally. They can answer queries, perform tasks, and even manage devices through voice commands.

In marketing, NLP has transformative applications. It enhances customer service by enabling more sophisticated and responsive chatbots that can handle complex customer queries. For instance, NLP allows bots to recognize when a customer is frustrated and might need to be transferred to a human agent.

NLP is invaluable in social media monitoring. It can analyze vast amounts of data from social media platforms to gauge public sentiment about a brand or product. This analysis helps marketers understand prevailing customer attitudes and can guide strategic decisions such as campaign adjustments or product improvements.

Furthermore, NLP helps personalize content. It studies how users engage with content to offer tailored suggestions, boosting user satisfaction and engagement.

NLP is not just about parsing and generating language; it's about understanding and engaging with consumers on a level that mimics human interaction, making it a critical technology in the evolving landscape of digital marketing. As this technology continues to advance, its integration into marketing strategies is expected to deepen, offering more nuanced and sophisticated ways to engage customers.

Let's dive into how Siri and Alexa, as AI technologies, have revolutionized marketing through their applications in voice-assisted interactions, setting a benchmark in the industry.

Siri and Alexa: Pioneers of Voice-Assisted Marketing

Siri, developed by Apple, and Alexa, from Amazon, are not just tools for setting reminders or playing music; they are sophisticated marketing platforms that have reshaped consumer interactions. These AI-powered assistants use advanced natural language processing (NLP) to understand and respond to user commands, making them integral to daily routines for millions of users worldwide.

Engaging Customers Through Personalized Marketing

Siri and Alexa have opened new avenues for personalized marketing directly through smart devices. By analyzing user queries and interactions, they offer personalized shopping suggestions, news updates, and entertainment options that align with the user's preferences and past behaviors. This level of personalization ensures that marketing messages delivered through these platforms are highly relevant and engaging.

Enhancing Brand Visibility and Interaction

These voice assistants also enhance brand visibility. For example, when users ask for the best skin care products, Siri and Alexa can suggest products from partnered brands, directly influencing consumer purchase decisions. This interaction not only boosts sales but also strengthens brand recall as users begin to associate brand names with convenience and personalized service.

Driving Innovation in Customer Service

Moreover, Siri and Alexa have transformed customer service by providing instant, on-demand assistance to user inquiries. Whether it's answering questions about a product or resolving issues, these assistants offer a seamless service experience that helps brands build trust and loyalty among consumers. Their ability to handle multiple service tasks without human intervention reduces wait times and improves overall customer satisfaction.

Collecting Valuable Consumer Insights

From a marketing perspective, the data collected through interactions with Siri and Alexa is invaluable. Each query and command provides insights into consumer preferences, habits, and trends, allowing companies to fine-tune their marketing strategies and product offerings. This data-driven approach helps companies stay ahead in highly competitive markets by adapting quickly to changing consumer needs.

Examples of Innovative Marketing Campaigns

A notable marketing campaign utilizing these voice assistants was when a major retailer integrated their product catalog with Alexa. Users could shop using voice commands, which not only simplified the shopping experience but also provided the retailer with insights into shopping habits and preferences. This integration led to an increase in customer engagement and sales, showcasing the practical benefits of incorporating AI technologies like Alexa and Siri into marketing strategies.

Chapter 3

Introduction to Leveraging AI for Enhanced Customer Interaction

Here's how a typical interaction might unfold between a customer and Amazon's AI chatbot while shopping for a camera:

Customer: Hi, I'm looking to upgrade to a professional camera for wildlife photography. Can you help?

Amazon Chatbot: Absolutely! Do you have any specific models in mind, or would you like some recommendations based on popular choices?

Customer: I'd appreciate some recommendations, please.

Amazon Chatbot: Sure thing! The Nikon D850 is highly recommended for wildlife photography due to its high resolution and fast autofocus. It also performs well in various lighting conditions. Would you like to know more about this model or see some alternatives?

Customer: That sounds good, but how does it perform in low-light conditions?

Amazon Chatbot: The Nikon D850 excels in low light with its ISO range of up to 102400, ensuring quality shots in dim environments. It's perfect for capturing dawn and dusk wildlife activities.

Customer: Great! Could you show me some reviews from other wildlife photographers?

Amazon Chatbot: Of course. [Shows reviews] Here's what others who have purchased the Nikon D850 specifically for wildlife photography have to say. They've noted its durability and excellent image quality in natural settings.

Customer: Thanks, that's very helpful. Can you add that to my cart, and maybe suggest a compatible lens for wildlife shots?

Amazon Chatbot: Done! I've added the Nikon D850 to your cart. For wildlife photography, I recommend the Nikon 70-200mm lens. It's great for capturing distant subjects with clarity. Shall I add this to your cart as well?

Customer: Yes, please, and include a sturdy tripod too.

Amazon Chatbot: All set! I've added the Nikon 70-200mm lens and a compatible tripod to your cart. You're all ready for a fantastic wildlife photography experience. Would you like to proceed to checkout?

Customer: Yes, let's check out.

Amazon Chatbot: Perfect! Here's your cart for review. When you're ready, just confirm, and we'll finalize your purchase. Thanks for shopping with us today!

Customer: Thanks for all your help!

The rise of AI-powered chatbots are changing the way businesses connect with their customers, making interactions quicker and more personal. These chatbots are available 24/7, which means they can answer questions, resolve issues, and provide assistance at any time. This is especially valuable because it ensures customers get help whenever they need it, without delays.

Chatbots can handle many conversations at once, which is a big advantage during busy periods like sales or product launches when there are lots of customer inquiries. They manage this heavy load without sacrificing the quality of service, ensuring every customer interaction is as good as the last.

These AI systems are not just about handling queries—they also make each interaction more personal. They learn from past conversations and use this data to make future interactions more relevant and helpful. For instance, if a chatbot knows you often buy science fiction books, it might recommend a newly released sci-fi novel during your next chat.

Using chatbots can also cut down on costs. They take care of routine questions and issues, allowing human customer service agents to focus on more complex problems. This can lead to fewer customer service staff or free them up to handle other important tasks. Chatbots also tend to handle inquiries faster, which means more issues are resolved in less time.

One of the best things about these chatbots is that they learn from every interaction. They use this information to continually improve their responses and become better at helping customers. However, businesses need to set these systems up correctly to ensure they can handle complicated issues or pass them to a human when necessary. Businesses also need to keep customer data safe, as chatbots often deal with personal information.

Predictive Analytics

Predictive analytics is like a crystal ball for marketers. It uses past data to guess what customers might buy in the future. This isn't just about guessing, though; it's about understanding patterns from what happened before and using those insights to make smart choices about what might happen next.

Think about a shop that knows it sells more umbrellas when it rains. Predictive analytics is like that shopkeeper but for all sorts of products and behaviors. It looks at lots of past data to see trends like maybe more people buying ice cream in July or gym memberships spiking in January. By seeing these patterns, marketers can prepare better, making sure they have the right products ready at the right times or setting up ads that hit just when you might need something.

This technology isn't just about selling more; it's also about making shopping feel more personal. If a store knows you often buy coffee, predictive analytics can remind you when you're likely running low or suggest a new blend you might enjoy. It's about making suggestions that are useful and timely, which can make shopping feel less like a work and more like a service.

Predictive analytics also helps stores manage their stock better. If a store knows what's likely to sell and when they can keep just enough on hand without overstocking or running out. This cuts down on waste and saves money, which is good for the company and good for prices. Predictive analytics isn't just for solving customer problems; it goes beyond by offering solutions.

Amazon, one of the world's largest online retailers, uses predictive analytics extensively to enhance the shopping experience for its millions of customers. They analyze data from previous purchases, searched items, items left in carts, and even how long you hover over a product. This data helps them predict what you might be interested in buying next.

For instance, if you've been searching for garden tools on Amazon, their predictive algorithms might start showing you related products like gardening gloves, seed packets, or even books about gardening. This isn't random; it's a calculated suggestion based on the behavior of thousands of customers who showed similar interests.

Here's how it benefits both the customer and Amazon:

Customer Convenience: The recommendations can help you find products that you might need without searching for them.

Increased Sales for Amazon: By showing relevant products, Amazon increases the chance that you'll make a purchase.

Amazon's system is so advanced that it can also predict what products will be in demand in different regions and manage its inventory accordingly to reduce shipping times and costs.

However, predictive analytics relies heavily on having high-quality data. Poor data can lead to incorrect predictions, which might frustrate customers rather than help them. Additionally, there's a big responsibility to handle this data ethically. Companies must ensure they comply with data protection laws like GDPR in Europe, which protects consumer data privacy.

Personalization at Scale

Personalization at scale is a transformative capability that AI brings to the world of marketing. By leveraging data from individual customer interactions and preferences, AI enables businesses to craft marketing messages that feel uniquely tailored to each person. Personalization algorithms have become the backbone of the digital world.

How AI Achieves Personalization at Scale?

AI systems analyze data from various customer interactions—such as past purchases, search queries, and browsing habits—to build detailed customer profiles. These profiles inform the AI on the best products, services, or messages to present to each customer. The AI can recognize patterns in the data that might not be obvious to human marketers, such as subtle preferences or emerging trends.

For example, a customer who frequently buys books from a particular genre might receive recommendations for new releases in that genre. But it goes beyond recommendations. AI can adjust the timing of emails, the layout of the website they see, and even the special offers or coupons they receive, all tailored to increase relevance and engagement.

Real-World Example

Spotify's approach to personalization through AI serves as an excellent example of how technology can tailor experiences at an individual level effectively. By analyzing vast amounts of data about a user's listening habits—including the genres they prefer, the songs they repeat, and even the time of day they listen—Spotify's

AI algorithms can create highly personalized playlists that resonate with each user's unique musical taste.

How Spotify's Personalization Works

Spotify uses several types of machine learning algorithms to understand and predict what music a user will enjoy. One of its most famous features, "Discover Weekly," is a playlist that updates every Monday with new songs that the user has never listened to on the platform but is likely to enjoy. This feature uses collaborative filtering models, which analyze both individual and collective user data to make these predictions.

The personalized playlists generated by Spotify's AI significantly enhance user engagement. Users discover music that they likely wouldn't have found on their own, which keeps them coming back to the platform each week. This ongoing engagement is crucial for Spotify's business model, which relies on keeping users interested and subscribed.

Spotify's AI-driven personalization also supports emerging artists by connecting their music with likely fans. This broadens the artists' reach and diversifies the music discovery experience for users.

Spotify's use of data for personalization raises important questions about privacy. The company must navigate the fine line between offering personalized experiences and respecting user privacy. Transparency about how data is collected, used, and protected is key to maintaining user trust.

Segmentation and Targeting

Segmentation and targeting are fundamental aspects of marketing that have been dramatically enhanced by AI, allowing businesses to identify and focus on the most relevant audience segments for their campaigns.

AI-driven segmentation involves using advanced algorithms to analyze large datasets and identify distinct groups within a customer base. These groups, or segments, are defined by shared characteristics such as demographics, purchasing behaviors, or interaction histories. Psychographic, customer behavioral, and targeting customers. Unlike traditional methods, which often rely on broader, less precise categories, AI can uncover nuanced patterns and micro-segments that might be invisible to human analysts.

Once segments are identified, AI enhances the targeting process. It enables marketers to craft messages that are precisely tailored to the preferences and needs of each segment. For example, AI can help a company recognize that a particular segment of its audience prefers eco-friendly products. The company can then specifically target these consumers with ads for their green products, significantly increasing the relevance of the message and the likelihood of engagement. This is a benefit to keeping customers engaged which can increase conversion rate and build brand loyalty.

The precision of AI-driven segmentation and targeting not only boosts the effectiveness of marketing campaigns and improves resource allocation. By focusing efforts on segments that are most likely to respond, businesses can reduce wastage on broad, untargeted campaigns. This targeted approach not only drives better outcomes and enhances customer satisfaction by reducing irrelevant marketing advertising.

The Future Is Here

Looking ahead, marketing is all about personalization. AI allows companies to tailor their communications so precisely that each customer can feel like the product or service is designed just for them. Whether it's suggesting products based on past purchases or sending messages at just the right time, AI helps businesses meet individual needs on a massive scale.

What's really exciting is how AI lets marketers focus more on the creative and emotional aspects of marketing. By handling routine tasks, AI frees up human employees to tackle projects that require more complex thinking and emotional intelligence. This blend of human creativity and AI efficiency is creating more meaningful and effective marketing strategies.

With great power comes great responsibility. The ability to gather and analyze extensive data requires a strong commitment to protecting privacy and ensuring fairness. Businesses need to be transparent about how they use AI and work hard to keep customer trust.

For businesses looking to keep up with the times, adopting AI is crucial. It can significantly enhance how they understand and interact with customers, ultimately leading to better customer satisfaction and loyalty. But it's important to move forward thoughtfully, always considering the ethical implications of using such powerful technology.

Chapter 4
AI-Driven Content and Communication

"Create an advertisement script for wheat bread that channels the distinctive style of Quentin Tarantino. The ad should feature dramatic, cinematic dialogue and a bold, edgy atmosphere, complete with sharp visuals and a compelling narrative that turns an ordinary product into something extraordinary. Include a memorable tagline at the end that captures the essence of the brand in a way that resonates with Tarantino's unique storytelling." – My Prompt.

[Opening Scene: A dimly-lit, retro-style kitchen with a checkerboard floor and vintage appliances. The camera zooms in on a rugged, charismatic chef with a tattoo sleeve, vigorously kneading dough on a flour-dusted counter.]

Chef (looking directly at the camera): "You think you know bread? Buddy, you haven't seen anything yet."

[Cut to, The dough is now a perfect loaf of wheat bread, going into an old-fashioned oven. Rockabilly music plays in the background.]

Voiceover (with a gritty, engaging tone): "In a world where everyone settles for the same old bland, we're firing up something that's anything but ordinary."

[Scene shifts: The bread emerges golden and steaming. The chef slams a large knife down next to it, slicing it with precision. Each slice falls in slow motion, the sound almost exaggerated.]

Chef (smirking): "This ain't your grandma's recipe. This is wheat bread with attitude. Made from grains that have seen more sunsets than you, baked with the kind of passion that movies are made of."

[Quick shots: Various people in different settings—a painter in a loft, a jazz musician in a smoky bar, a writer in a cluttered study—all enjoying the bread with various toppings.]

Voiceover: "It's the choice for those who lead, not follow. For the dreamers, the rebels, the artists. This bread fuels the bold."

[Final shot: The chef holds up a piece with a pat of butter melting into it.]

Chef: "So, what do you say? Ready to taste something legendary?"

[Text flashes on the screen with a stylized font:]

"Quentin's Cut Wheat Bread — Bold. Artisan. Unapologetic."

The tagline on screen as the music hits a crescendo: "Eat Boldly."

The advertisement script for wheat bread, styled like a Quentin Tarantino movie, was actually generated with ChatGPT. This example shows how AI can automatically create tailored content to fit specific styles or themes.

Automated Content Creation

Automated content creation through AI is a transformative technology in many fields, especially in marketing and media. This process involves programming AI systems to produce written content, videos, audio, and images specifically aligned with individual preferences. AI can generate dynamic social media posts with customized messages, images, and offers based on user behavior and interest.

How It Works

AI tools use algorithms to analyze user data such as past behavior, engagement history, and personal preferences. By understanding what content engages a user, AI can produce new content that is likely to be

The advertisement script for wheat bread, styled like a Quentin Tarantino movie, was actually generated with ChatGPT. This example highlights the potential of AI in automated content creation, where it can tailor content to specific themes or styles.

Exploring Automated Content Creation with AI

Automated content creation through AI is revolutionizing the way content is produced across various industries, particularly in marketing, Journalism, entertainment, and many more. AI systems are designed to generate written materials, videos, audio, and images, all customized to align with user preferences and historical data.

Understanding How AI Creates Content:

AI-powered tools are equipped with algorithms that analyze extensive data about users' interactions, preferences, and engagement. This data informs the AI about which types of content resonate most with a particular user or audience segment. For instance, if a user frequently reads and interacts with adventure stories, the AI might generate similar themes in the content it creates for that user.

Applications in Real-World Settings

In the era of the digital marketing world, AI-driven content creation allows companies to design personalized advertising campaigns, social media posts, and promotional videos. The content is tailored to the audience's interests and optimized for engagement, increasing the effectiveness of marketing strategies. For example, an online retailer could use AI to generate product descriptions that are styled to match the linguistic preferences of different customer segments and target markets.

The Benefits of AI in Content Creation

For businesses, the advantages of AI in content creation include:

- **Efficiency:** AI can produce content at a scale and speed that humans cannot match.

- **Relevance:** Content is more likely to engage and convert when it is deeply aligned with the audience's preferences.

- **Cost-effectiveness:** Reducing the need for human content creators can lower costs significantly.

Despite the benefits, there are challenges to consider. The quality of AI-generated content heavily depends on the data used to train the AI models. Poor data can lead to content that is irrelevant or even inappropriate. Additionally, there are concerns about data privacy and the potential for AI to perpetuate biases if not carefully monitored.

As AI technology continues to advance, automated content creation is expected to become even more sophisticated. This could lead to AI not just emulating human content creation but also innovating new forms of content that could inspire creativity among human artists and writers.

Enhancing SEO with AI Tools

SEO is all about making your website more visible when people search for products or services related to your business in search engines like Google. AI significantly improves this process by analyzing large amounts of data and predicting what changes can make your content more attractive to search engines.

How AI Enhances SEO

AI tools process large amounts of data from your website and other sources to understand how users interact with your content and what drives them to your site. This might include analyzing keywords, the time spent on various pages, bounce rates, and more. By aggregating this data, AI can identify patterns and trends that might not be visible through manual analysis.

Using historical data and machine learning algorithms, AI can predict which changes to your website might improve SEO performance. For example, AI can suggest updates to your meta descriptions, headlines, or content that are more likely to resonate with both search engines and users based on current trends and search engine algorithms.

AI enables dynamic customization of content to suit different user segments. By analyzing user behavior, AI can adjust the content displayed to different visitors, making it more relevant to their interests and geographical location. This kind of personalization not only improves user experience but also signals to search engines that your website is highly relevant, which can boost your rankings.

AI tools can automatically make adjustments to your SEO strategies based on real-time data. For instance, if an AI system notices that certain types of content are performing better than others, it can shift focus to increase the visibility of that content or replicate its style in other areas.

AI can help improve website navigation, speed up page load times, and make the site easier to crawl for search engines—all of which are crucial SEO factors. Improving these technical SEO aspects not only helps with rankings but also enhances the overall user experience, reducing bounce rates and increasing time spent on the site.

An example of AI-driven SEO is seen in large e-commerce platforms like Amazon, which use AI to optimize their vast product listings for search engines. Amazon's AI analyzes customer reviews, questions, and behavior to optimize product descriptions and improve search rankings. This ensures that when customers search for specific products, they find what they are looking for quickly and easily, which in turn improves Amazon's organic search performance.

Let's dive deeper into how AI-powered SEO software like CanIRank optimizes website content for better search engine performance.

Detailed Look at CanIRank

CanIRank is an AI-driven SEO tool that stands out by not just providing data but by offering actionable recommendations. Here's how it specifically helps in enhancing a website's SEO:

CanIRank starts by thoroughly analyzing the content on your website. It looks at factors such as keyword usage, content structure, and readability. But it doesn't stop there.

The software then compares your content with that of your competitors, especially those ranking higher in search engine results. This comparison isn't just about keywords but also includes backlink strength, content length, and other SEO metrics.

Based on this comprehensive analysis, CanIRank provides specific suggestions on what changes can be made to improve rankings. For example, it might suggest increasing the length of the content, using certain keywords more frequently, or improving the meta descriptions and titles.

What makes CanIRank particularly useful is its ability to predict the impact of recommended changes. This means it can forecast how likely it is that implementing a particular suggestion will improve your search rankings.

After the changes are made, CanIRank continues to monitor the site's performance and suggest further adjustments. This ongoing optimization process helps in keeping the website competitive as search algorithms and market dynamics evolve.

Businesses using CanIRank have seen measurable improvements in their search engine rankings. By following specific, data-driven recommendations, these businesses can make informed decisions that lead to better visibility and more organic traffic. For instance, an e-commerce site might find that after adjusting its product descriptions and titles based on CanIRank's suggestions, it starts ranking higher for key product search terms, driving more potential customers to its pages.

Example of AI Success in SEO

Let's talk about how a big travel website like Expedia uses AI to make sure people who are planning trips find exactly what they need on their site. Expedia has tons of pages about different travel destinations, tips, and deals. To make it easier for travelers to find useful information, Expedia uses AI to sift through search trends and what customers are currently interested in.

When someone searches for something travel-related, AI helps Expedia figure out which of their pages are likely to be most useful based on what people are looking for at that moment. For example, if there's a sudden increase in searches for "beach vacations in Florida," the AI notes this trend and helps push content related to Florida beaches higher up in search results. This makes it more likely for someone searching for a beach vacation to come across Expedia's recommendations and offers.

What's really smart about this approach is how Expedia's AI continuously learns and updates. It looks at how people interact with the search results—like which articles they click on and how long they stay on a page. This feedback tells the AI if it's doing a good job or if it needs to change which pages it suggests for certain searches.

By keeping its content well-aligned with what potential travelers are looking for, Expedia makes its website easier to use and stays competitive in search engine rankings. This means more people clicking through to their site organically, without Expedia having to pay for ads to get their attention. It's a win for the travelers who find what they need quickly and a win for Expedia, which gets more visitors to its site.

How AI Optimizes Advertising

AI is transforming advertising by optimizing ad placements and content to maximize engagement rates. This capability of AI is particularly significant in the digital marketing space, where capturing and maintaining consumer attention is crucial.

AI technologies in advertising are designed to analyze vast amounts of consumer data—such as past purchases, browsing history, and interaction with previous ads—to tailor advertisements according to individual preferences and behaviors. This tailored approach ensures that ads are relevant and presented at the optimal time and place to catch the consumer's interest. Additionally, if you struggle to come up with ideas for a copy at all, AI can be a lifesaver.

AI can determine the best times to display ads based on when users are most active online and which platforms they frequent. It can also predict which type of ad content—whether video, image, or text—will resonate more effectively with different segments of the audience.

Dynamic Ad Insertion

AI is changing the advertising game with something called dynamic ad insertion. This smart technology lets streaming platforms show ads that are really well-suited to each viewer. So, when you're watching your favorite shows, the ads you see are picked by AI to match your interests.

For example, imagine you're watching a lot of cooking shows. With dynamic ad insertion, the AI takes this cue, and next time you might see an ad for a new kitchen gadget or a gourmet food delivery service right in the middle of your show. What's clever here is that the AI chooses these ads based on what you like to watch, so the ads feel more relevant and less disruptive.

This kind of advertising is great for businesses because their ads are more likely to be seen by people who are genuinely interested in what they're offering. It's also a win for viewers because the ads they see are about things they might actually want to know more about, rather than random products.

In essence, dynamic ad insertion by AI makes watching ads a less annoying experience. You get ads that may actually be useful, and companies get to show their products to the people most likely to be interested in them. It's a smarter way to do advertising that's good for everyone involved.

The immediate benefit of this AI-driven strategy is a higher engagement rate, as ads are more likely to appeal to the interests of the viewer. Additionally, AI optimization helps companies achieve a better return on investment (ROI) on their advertising spend by reducing waste through misdirected ads. It also enhances the user experience by making ads less intrusive and more relevant, which can lead to increased customer satisfaction and loyalty.

AI is revolutionizing advertising by enabling businesses to create more personalized and effective ad campaigns. For example, **Coca-Cola** partnered with OpenAI to run a creative contest using AI tools like ChatGPT and DALL-E, engaging users to create art based on historic ads. **Calm** used AI through Amazon's Personalize tool to recommend content that matches user preferences, improving engagement. **BMW** integrated AI-generated art into their campaigns, showcasing their luxury cars while emotionally connecting with their audience.

Ethical Considerations and Challenges

When we talk about using AI in advertising, especially with techniques like personalized ads, there's a whole world of ethical considerations and challenges that come into play. The main issue revolves around how much personal data is being used and how it's handled. Let's break this down in a simple way.

Imagine you're browsing online, and you start noticing that every ad seems to know exactly what you've been searching for—whether it's a vacation spot or a new pair of shoes. That's AI working in the background, using data you've provided through your searches and website visits. While it can feel like magic to see just what you were looking for, it also raises big questions about privacy.

Here's where the ethical challenges come in. Companies have to be very careful about how they collect and use this data. They need to make sure they're not invading your privacy or making you feel uncomfortable with the amount of personal detail they seem to know. This is crucial because trust is a big part of customer relationships. If people feel like their data is being misused, they might start avoiding certain brands or platforms.

Furthermore, there's the law to consider. In places like Europe, there's something called the GDPR—General Data Protection Regulation—which sets strict rules about how personal data can be used. Companies have to be transparent about what data they're collecting and why, and they need to get clear consent from customers before using that data for advertising.

In a nutshell, while AI in advertising can make ads more relevant and effective, companies need to handle personal data with great care to maintain trust and comply with legal requirements. This careful balancing act between using data for business advantages and respecting privacy is at the heart of the ethical considerations around AI in advertising.

Chapter 5
AI in Marketing Operations

AI-Crafted Marketing Email Example:

Subject: Unlock Your Style Adventures with Our Exclusive Spring Collection!

Hello,

Spring is in the air, and it's time to rejuvenate your wardrobe with pieces that are as vibrant as the season! Our brand new Spring Collection has just blossomed, and we're excited to give you a first look at the stunning styles waiting just for you.

Why You'll Love This Collection:

Fresh Floral Prints: Perfect for picnics in the park or weekend getaways.

Light & Airy Fabrics: Stay cool and chic on those sunny spring days.

Exclusive Subscriber Discounts: Enjoy a special 20% off your first purchase from the collection.

But hurry! Your exclusive preview ends this Sunday. Use code SPRINGFLING at checkout to claim your discount.

Shop Now | Explore the Collection

See you in the sunshine,

With Regards

AI-Crafted Social Media Content Example: Instagram Post

🌷✨ Step into spring with style! ✨🌷

Our much-anticipated Spring Collection is here, and it's blooming with possibilities. From breezy dresses to eye-catching florals, find your perfect spring look and embrace the new season with confidence!

👗 #SpringIntoStyle #FreshFinds

👉 Swipe to see our top picks!

🛍️ Tap to shop the collection!

The email and social media content above was generated with Cloud AI, showcasing how artificial intelligence can craft engaging and personalized marketing messages. Now, let's explore how AI takes this capability even further through marketing automation.

Marketing Automation Powered by AI

Marketing automation has revolutionized how businesses interact with their customers. Powered by AI, this technology automates and optimizes routine marketing tasks, ensuring that communications like emails and social media posts are not only timely but also highly targeted and relevant.

What is Marketing Automation?

Marketing automation refers to the software and technologies designed to market more effectively on multiple channels online (such as email, social media, and websites) and automate repetitive tasks. AI enhances these processes by adding a layer of intelligence that predicts customer behaviors, personalizes messages, and manages the timing of marketing communications without human intervention.

Key Functions of AI in Marketing Automation

AI-driven marketing automation significantly enhances how businesses interact with customers by personalizing the entire communication process. Here's a deeper look into how AI helps with scheduling posts, segmenting contacts, and sending targeted emails, all automatically:

Scheduling Posts: AI systems can predict the best times to post on various social media platforms by analyzing historical engagement data. For instance, if the data shows that most of your audience engages with your content in the evening, the AI will schedule posts during these peak times to maximize visibility and interaction. This means businesses can ensure their posts have the highest chance of being seen without constantly monitoring social media trends themselves.

Segmenting Contacts: AI takes customer segmentation to a new level by using advanced data analysis techniques. It looks at customer behavior, preferences, and even sentiment expressed in past interactions to group similar customers together. This allows for incredibly focused marketing efforts. For example, if an AI system identifies a group of customers who frequently purchase children's books, it can segment these contacts into a 'young parents' category, who might then receive more targeted emails about family-friendly products or upcoming sales on children's books.

Sending Targeted Emails: Once AI has segmented the contacts, it can also automate the process of sending personalized emails to each segment. By analyzing what each group or individual prefers or needs based on their past interactions and purchase history, AI can tailor emails to match these preferences. This might mean sending a personalized coupon for a product a customer has looked at but not purchased, or sending product updates that align with their interests.

Scenario

Reader's Haven has a diverse customer base and a wide range of book genres. They want to ensure that their marketing emails and social media posts reach the right customers at the right time with content that appeals to their specific interests.

Implementation of AI-Driven Marketing Automation

Scheduling Social Media Posts

AI Analysis: The AI system analyzes past engagement data across various social media platforms to identify peak times when specific customer segments are most active.

Action Taken: Based on this analysis, AI schedules posts about new romance novels at 7 PM on Facebook, as data shows that fans of this genre are most active during this time. Similarly, posts about business books are scheduled for weekday mornings on LinkedIn when professional users are more likely to browse.

Segmenting Email Contacts

AI Analysis: The AI reviews purchase histories and clicks from past emails to segment the customers into groups such as "Young Adult Readers," "History Enthusiasts," and "Sci-Fi Fans."

Action Taken: Each segment receives customized emails. For instance, "Sci-Fi Fans" get early notifications about new sci-fi releases and author interviews, enhancing their engagement with content tailored to their preferences.

Sending Targeted Emails

AI Analysis: The system continuously updates customer profiles based on their interactions with the website and email content.

Action Taken: If a customer frequently views pages related to children's books but hasn't made a purchase, the AI sends a targeted email with a special discount on popular children's books. This email is personalized, addressing the customer by name and referencing their interest, making the content highly relevant.

By implementing these AI-driven strategies, Readers' Haven not only increases the efficiency of their marketing efforts but also significantly boosts customer engagement and satisfaction. Their marketing emails see higher open and click-through rates because they resonate more with recipients' interests. Social media engagement increases as posts are optimized for times when target audiences are most active online.

Benefits of AI-Driven Marketing Automation

The benefits of AI-driven marketing automation are transforming how businesses interact with their customers, optimize their workflows, and improve their return on investment (ROI). Here's a detailed look at each benefit:

Increased Efficiency

AI in marketing automation streamlines a variety of tasks that traditionally required significant manual input. By automating processes like data analysis, lead scoring, and even basic customer communication, AI frees up marketing teams to focus on more strategic and creative tasks. For example, AI can analyze thousands of data points from user interactions to identify trends and patterns much quicker than a human could. This capability allows marketing teams to quickly adjust campaigns based on real-time data, making the entire process more efficient.

Enhanced Personalization

AI takes personalization in marketing to a new level. Beyond inserting a customer's name in an email, AI analyzes individual user behavior to tailor marketing messages according to each customer's preferences and previous interactions. This could mean suggesting products similar to those they have shown interest in or sending them promotional offers at times they are most likely to make a purchase. By catering to the individual needs and preferences of each user, AI helps create a more personalized, engaging experience that is more likely to convert.

Improved ROI

By ensuring that marketing efforts are not wasted on uninterested parties, AI-driven automation significantly enhances the efficiency of marketing campaigns. AI helps in identifying the most effective marketing strategies and optimizing the allocation of resources based on performance data. This targeted approach reduces costs by minimizing wasted efforts and improves the overall return on investment by focusing on tactics that yield the best results. For example, AI can optimize ad spend by reallocating the budget in real-time to the most performing ads or audiences, ensuring that the marketing spend is always optimized for the best possible return.

Improving Marketing Efficiency with AI

AI revolutionizes marketing efficiency by providing deep insights into data that would take humans much longer to analyze. This speed in data processing allows for agile responses to market changes and consumer behavior, ensuring that marketing strategies remain effective and responsive.

Real-World Application

Take the example of a large retail company that implements AI to analyze customer feedback across multiple platforms. AI tools quickly sift through thousands of customer reviews, social media mentions, and direct feedback to identify common themes and sentiments. This rapid analysis helps the company understand the public perception of a new product launch much faster than traditional methods.

Using predictive analytics, AI can forecast trends and shifts in consumer preferences. This allows marketing teams to adjust their campaigns in real time. For instance, if AI detects a growing interest in eco-friendly products in real-time data, the marketing team can immediately increase the visibility of their sustainable products in online ads and social media posts.

AI also simplifies complex decision-making processes. By providing actionable insights and clear analytics, AI helps marketing teams make informed decisions quickly. This capability is crucial when navigating fast-paced markets where delays can mean missed opportunities.

AI optimizes marketing spend by identifying the most effective channels and tactics for engaging the target audience. For example, if AI analysis shows that video content on social media yields four times the engagement of other content types for a particular demographic, a company can allocate more resources to video production and distribution, ensuring better ROI.

AI's ability to handle vast amounts of data comes into play in personalizing customer interactions. By understanding individual customer behaviors and preferences, AI can tailor marketing messages and offers, enhancing the customer experience and increasing the likelihood of conversion. By integrating AI into their marketing strategies, companies not only enhance operational efficiency but also gain a competitive edge by being able to respond quickly and effectively to changing market dynamics.

Case Example

Patagonia, an outdoor clothing company known for its commitment to sustainability, effectively uses AI to enhance its marketing efforts, making its operations more efficient and boosting its return on investment in a unique and engaging way.

Patagonia uses AI to really understand what their customers care about, like keeping things eco-friendly and making sure their gear lasts a long time. This smart tech looks at all the different ways customers interact with Patagonia—like what they buy, what they say in reviews, and what they seem to care about on social media.

With this info, Patagonia can send out emails that feel really personal. For instance, if someone buys a lot of hiking gear, they might get a special email from Patagonia talking all about their new, sustainable hiking products. They'd explain how these products are made with the environment in mind, showing pictures or videos that help the customer see the good they're doing by choosing these items.

Patagonia's interactive AI-driven campaigns are a clever blend of technology and storytelling that really engage customers by showing them where and how their products are made. For instance, they have a feature called the "Footprint Chronicles" which allows customers to track the impact of a Patagonia product from design through delivery. This interactive tool on their website shows detailed maps and gives information about the factories, the workers, and the environmental practices at each stage of the production process.

In these campaigns, when a customer clicks on different parts of the product story, the content adjusts dynamically. This means if a customer shows a lot of interest in the environmental aspects, the AI might show more detailed information about Patagonia's recycling processes or its use of renewable energy.

This approach does more than just sell clothes; it educates people about sustainability and the importance of ethical manufacturing.

For instance, if a customer buys a winter jacket, Patagonia's AI takes note of this purchase and considers what other items might be useful for the customer as the colder months approach.

Here's how they might tailor offers specifically:

Complementary Product Suggestions: After purchasing a winter jacket, the customer might receive recommendations for thermal leggings or eco-friendly wool socks. This suggestion isn't random; it's based on the likelihood that someone preparing for cold weather might also need these items.

Seasonal Promotions: Patagonia's AI can identify when winter is approaching based on the customer's location. It then sends personalized emails or notifications about products that are essential for the season, like warm clothing or waterproof gear, often including a special promotion or discount as an incentive.

Re-engagement Offers: If the customer showed interest in certain products by browsing but didn't make a purchase, Patagonia's AI might send a follow-up email a few weeks later, perhaps offering a discount or highlighting the benefits of the product, like its sustainability features or durability, which align with the customer's values and previous interest patterns.

Impact of AI on Marketing ROI

Businesses that implement AI-driven personalized marketing strategies typically see a significant improvement in engagement and sales conversions. This is due to the targeted nature of the communications, which ensures that marketing efforts resonate more effectively with interested customers, thus optimizing advertising spend.

For a company like Patagonia, known for its commitment to sustainability and ethical practices, AI-enhanced marketing likely helps to strengthen customer loyalty and attract new customers who value these principles. These strategies likely contribute to:

Increased Customer Retention: Personalized marketing makes customers feel understood and valued, which increases their loyalty and likelihood of repeat purchases.

Higher Conversion Rates: By targeting users with personalized offers and products they are likely to be interested in, Patagonia likely sees higher conversion rates from its marketing efforts.

Cost Efficiency: AI-driven targeting reduces waste by focusing resources on the most promising customer interactions, improving overall marketing efficiency and ROI.

The Human Touch in a Digital Age

AI in marketing does a lot more than just handle numbers and data. It helps us connect with people better. Imagine you're using AI to find out what your customers really like and what they need before they even tell you. This means you can talk to them in a way that feels more personal and caring.

Here's how it works: AI looks at all the interactions customers have with your emails, your website, or your ads. It learns what they like, what they don't like, and even how they feel about certain things. Then, it uses this information to help you make your messages more personal. For example, if someone spends a lot of time looking at running shoes on your website, AI can help you send them an email that talks about those shoes and maybe offers a special deal.

But it's not just about selling things. It's about making connections. When customers feel that a brand really understands them and gives them what they need, they're more likely to stick with that brand. AI helps make sure that every message feels like it's coming from a friend who knows what they like. This makes customers happy and helps build trust between them and the brand.

So, in a digital world where everything can seem a bit cold and automatic, AI brings a human touch. It helps businesses talk to their customers like people, not just numbers on a screen.

Chapter 6
Emotional Intelligence and AI

"Imagine waking up and finding out that your AI assistant, Alex, has detected a problem your customers are facing. Alex has been keeping an eye on customer interactions all night."

Scenario: AI's Emotional Intelligence in Action at "KopiLah"

KopiLah, a popular coffee delivery service in Malaysia, uses an AI assistant named Alex to understand customer feelings. One morning, Alex notices a lot of negative comments about the quality of the latest batch of coffee beans.

Alex looks at social media posts, customer reviews, and feedback. It finds comments like, "The coffee beans in my last order were not fresh," and "I am unhappy with the recent delivery." Alex not only sees these comments but also understands the feelings behind them, marking them as negative.

Alex quickly informs the customer service team. The team reaches out to each unhappy customer with personalized apologies and offers. They might offer a refund, a replacement, or a discount on their next purchase. Each response is friendly and addresses the specific problem.

Customer Service Example Response: "Hi Faizal, we're really sorry to hear that the coffee beans you bought were not fresh. We're sending you a new batch of coffee beans right away. Please enjoy a 20% discount on your next order with us. Thank you for letting us know."

Besides addressing individual complaints, Alex's insights help the marketing team take broader actions. They post updates on social media to acknowledge the problem and explain the steps being taken to fix it. They also send an email to all recent customers, offering a small discount on their next purchase to regain their trust.

Social Media Post Example: "We've heard your feedback about the quality of our coffee beans, and we're taking immediate steps to ensure it doesn't happen again. Thank you for your patience and understanding. Enjoy a 10% discount on your next purchase with the code THANKYOU10."

Email Example: "Dear Customer, we've received your feedback about the quality of our coffee beans. We're addressing this issue to make sure it doesn't happen again. As a thank you for your patience, please enjoy a 10% discount on your next order with the code THANKYOU10."

Customers appreciate the quick and caring responses. They see that KopiLah is genuinely concerned about their satisfaction. Negative comments start to decline, and positive feedback begins to come in, with many customers praising the company for its excellent customer service.

Customer Feedback Example: "Thanks to KopiLah for quickly addressing my complaint about the coffee beans. Got a fresh batch today, and it tastes great! Fantastic customer service."

This shows how Alex's emotional intelligence helps KopiLah quickly understand and respond to customer issues. By using AI, KopiLah can improve customer satisfaction and maintain trust, ensuring every interaction feels personal and valued. This approach solves immediate problems and builds long-term customer loyalty.

Understanding Sentiment Analysis

Every human has sentiments and expressions. These are the emotions and feelings we show when we talk, write, or share our thoughts. AI can understand these emotions using a method called sentiment analysis. It looks at what people say on social media, in reviews, and in customer feedback to figure out their emotions. Here's how it works in simple terms:

Data Collection

AI collects data from various sources. This includes social media posts, customer reviews on websites, and direct feedback from surveys or customer service interactions. For example, AI might gather tweets about a new product launch or comments left on a product review site.

Text Analysis

Once the data is collected, AI reads through the text to find words and phrases that show emotions. Words like "happy," "love," or "great" are positive, while words like "angry," "bad," or "disappointed" are negative. For instance, if a customer review says, "I love how this coffee tastes!" AI marks this as positive.

Understanding Context

AI doesn't just count positive and negative words. It also looks at the context to understand the true meaning. For example, the sentence "The coffee was not bad" is positive even though it has the word "bad." AI learns to understand these subtle meanings.

Classifying Emotions

After analyzing the text, AI determines the overall emotion. It can tell if the sentiment is positive, negative, or neutral. This helps businesses understand how customers feel about their products or services. For example, if many reviews are positive, the company knows their product is well-received. If the reviews are negative, they know there might be a problem to fix.

Why Sentiment Analysis is Important

Understanding human emotions is key to connecting with people. Sentiment analysis helps AI understand these emotions by analyzing what customers say in reviews, social media posts, and feedback. This understanding helps businesses build strong relationships with their customers.

When companies know how customers feel, they can quickly address any issues. If a customer feels disappointed and shares their feelings online, AI can detect this emotion immediately. The company can then respond quickly, offering an apology and a solution. This shows the customer that the company cares about their satisfaction and is willing to make things right. Fixing problems quickly not only helps individual customers but also stops negative experiences from spreading.

Knowing customer emotions also helps businesses create better marketing campaigns. If customers like a specific feature of a product, the company can highlight this feature in their ads. This makes the marketing more effective because it focuses on what customers already value. On the other hand, if there's something customers don't like, the company can avoid promoting it and work on **product** improvements. By understanding customer emotions, businesses can create messages that connect more deeply with their *target audience*, leading to higher engagement and increased sales.

Engaging with customers on an emotional level builds trust and loyalty. When companies respond to feedback, it shows they listen and care. If a customer points out a mistake and the company takes steps to fix it, the customer feels valued. This builds loyalty because the customer sees that their opinions matter and that the company wants to improve their experience. These positive interactions turn customers into advocates who share their good experiences with others, attracting new customers and strengthening the brand's reputation.

Sentiment analysis helps businesses understand and respond to customer emotions effectively. This improves customer satisfaction, makes marketing strategies more impactful, and builds stronger, more loyal relationships with customers. This approach helps address immediate issues and contributes to long-term success and growth.

Research on AI Learning Emotions

Understanding human emotions is crucial for building effective AI systems. Around the world, researchers are developing advanced methods to teach AI how to recognize and respond to human emotions accurately. Here's a detailed look at some of the ongoing research in this field.

One key aspect of improving AI's ability to understand emotions is the creation of large, diverse datasets. Researchers are gathering data that reflects natural emotional expressions from multiple sources, such as facial expressions, voice tones, and text. This data helps train AI models to recognize a wide range of emotional cues accurately.

To enhance the accuracy of emotion recognition, researchers are refining multimodal fusion technology. This involves integrating information from various sources like facial expressions, speech, and written text. By combining these different types of data, AI can get a more complete understanding of human emotions. For example, if a person's voice sounds happy, but their words are negative, AI can analyze both cues to determine the true emotion.

In addition to relying on data, researchers are incorporating expert knowledge into AI systems to improve their emotional intelligence. This helps AI understand the context and nuances of human emotions better, especially in situations where data might be limited or ambiguous. For instance, integrating psychological theories can help AI systems interpret complex emotional responses more accurately.

Affective computing is a field that combines neuroscience with AI to measure and regulate emotional states using brain signals. Researchers are developing brain-computer interfaces that can detect a person's emotional state through neurological signals. This technology has potential applications in areas like clinical diagnostics, therapy, and even enhancing user experiences in virtual reality.

Creating more human-like interactions is another goal of emotion research. AI systems are being designed to engage in empathic dialogues by leveraging emotional cues from users. This is particularly useful in applications like elderly care, where AI can provide companionship and support by understanding and responding to the emotional needs of users.

The ability to process and analyze emotions in real time is becoming increasingly important. Researchers are developing algorithms that can handle large volumes of data quickly without losing accuracy. This allows businesses to respond to customer sentiments immediately, improving customer service and satisfaction.

Countries like China and India are leading the way in transforming the global research landscape in affective computing. These nations are investing heavily in creating extensive collaborations and setting standards for ethical norms in emotion recognition technology. Their efforts are pushing the boundaries of what AI can achieve in understanding human emotions.

Real-World Example

Consider how a large retail company like Walmart might use sentiment analysis. Suppose Walmart launches a new line of organic foods. AI scans social media and customer reviews to gather opinions. If many customers say things like, "I love the new organic options at Walmart!" the AI notes this positive sentiment. If others say, "The new organic products are too expensive," the AI captures this concern.

With this information, Walmart can adjust its strategy. They might run promotions to make the organic products more affordable or highlight the benefits to justify the price. By understanding and responding to customer emotions, Walmart can improve customer satisfaction and loyalty.

Personal and Responsive

Sentiment analysis allows AI to understand the emotions behind customer feedback, which helps in crafting marketing messages that feel personal and engaging. By analyzing sentiments from various sources like social media, reviews, and direct feedback, AI can tailor responses to match the emotional tone of the customer.

When AI detects positive sentiments, it can generate messages that reinforce and enhance the customer's positive experience. This could involve sending appreciative messages that make the customer feel valued and understood. Positive reinforcement helps in maintaining and strengthening customer satisfaction.

In cases of negative sentiment, AI can craft responses that show empathy and address the customer's concerns. By recognizing the issues highlighted by the customer, AI can provide solutions or compensatory offers that aim to resolve the problem and restore customer trust. This empathetic approach helps in mitigating negative feelings and turning a potentially bad experience into a positive resolution.

AI's ability to personalize interactions extends beyond addressing current sentiments. It can remember past interactions and preferences, allowing it to tailor future communications to the individual needs and interests of each customer. This ongoing personalization makes customers feel special and recognized, fostering a deeper connection with the brand.

Real-time sentiment analysis enables companies to respond quickly to customer feedback. Immediate responses to both positive and negative sentiments demonstrate attentiveness and care, enhancing the overall customer experience. This prompt action can significantly improve customer perception and loyalty.

By continuously learning from interactions, AI can refine its understanding of customer emotions and preferences, making each subsequent interaction more precise and personal. This continuous improvement cycle ensures that marketing messages remain relevant and effective, adapting to the evolving needs and emotions of the customers.

Enhancing Customer Service

Customer service is where companies connect with their customers, solve problems, and build relationships. Traditionally, this connection happened through face-to-face interactions. Customers talked to friendly staff who listened to their concerns, empathized with their issues, and offered solutions. This personal touch made customers feel valued and heard. However, with the advent of AI, this dynamic has changed.

AI-driven tools have transformed customer service by offering real-time, efficient communication. These tools can quickly analyze a customer's query, understand the context and emotion, and provide a relevant response. This speed and efficiency can be very satisfying for customers, especially when they need quick answers. AI can handle multiple inquiries at once, ensuring no customer is left waiting. It learns from each interaction, becoming better at predicting and addressing customer needs over time.

But this shift towards AI in customer service brings emotional complexities. Imagine a customer dealing with a frustrating issue. Speaking to a human who can empathize with their frustration, offer a kind word, and genuinely assure them that their problem will be resolved can be immensely comforting. AI, despite its capabilities, often lacks this emotional depth. It can recognize and respond to emotions to a certain extent, but it doesn't truly feel them. This can make interactions feel impersonal, even if the service is efficient.

Moreover, there is a growing concern about AI taking over jobs traditionally held by humans. Many customer service representatives worry about their job security as companies increasingly adopt AI solutions. The emotional toll of this transition is significant. Employees who have spent years honing their interpersonal skills and building customer relationships may feel undervalued and anxious about their future. This anxiety isn't just about losing a job; it's about losing a role where they make a difference in people's lives daily.

Customers, too, can feel the impact of this shift. While some appreciate the efficiency of AI, others miss the human connection. A machine might solve their problem quickly, but it doesn't replace the warmth of a friendly conversation or the reassurance of speaking to someone who genuinely understands their frustration. This lack of human touch can sometimes make customers feel isolated and unimportant, even if their issues are resolved.

In real-time communication, the stakes are even higher. An AI can provide quick solutions, but in moments of real frustration or emotional distress, the absence of a human touch can worsen a customer's negative feelings. For instance, if someone is dealing with a significant issue and is met with automated responses, they might feel that their concerns are not truly being heard, leading to greater dissatisfaction.

Despite these challenges, it's essential to remember that AI is a tool designed to assist, not replace, human workers. The goal of AI in customer service is to handle routine inquiries and provide quick solutions, freeing up human representatives to deal with more complex and emotionally charged issues. This collaboration between AI and human workers can create a more balanced and effective customer service experience. AI can handle quick, straightforward tasks, ensuring customers get timely responses, while human representatives can focus on providing the empathy and understanding that only a person can offer.

AI's Role in Emotion Management

AI has changed many aspects of our lives, from how we shop to how we communicate. But as AI becomes more advanced, especially in understanding and managing emotions, it raises important questions. Some people worry about giving machines too much control over our emotions. They ask if AI could end up ruling the world or causing harm if misused.

There are real concerns about AI managing emotions. One worry is that we might lose control over our lives. If machines can understand and influence our emotions, they might manipulate us in ways that are not in our best interest. For example, AI could create highly persuasive ads that make us buy things we don't need. This loss of control can make people feel uneasy and vulnerable.

Another big concern is the potential misuse of AI by those with bad intentions. If AI tools become widely accessible, they could be used to spread false information, manipulate public opinion, or even carry out cyber attacks. This misuse could lead to significant social and political problems, as well as personal harm. It's a scary thought that technology meant to help us could be turned against us.

Using AI to understand and manage emotions also brings up ethical and privacy issues. Collecting and analyzing data about people's feelings and behaviors can be invasive. There's a risk that this sensitive information could be used unethically or without people's consent. We need to think about how much of our personal lives we're willing to share with machines.

Despite these concerns, it's important to remember that AI is just a tool. Its impact depends on how we choose to use it. AI can be incredibly helpful when used for good purposes. It can improve customer service, make healthcare more personalized, enhance learning experiences, and much more. For example, AI can help doctors diagnose and treat diseases more accurately by analyzing patients' emotional states alongside their physical symptoms.

Blaming AI entirely for potential negative outcomes isn't fair. Like any other technological advancement, the responsibility lies with humans to use it ethically and wisely. Just as we regulate other powerful technologies, we need to create frameworks and policies that ensure AI is used for positive outcomes. We have the power to guide its development in a way that benefits society.

AI represents the next big step in technological evolution. Its potential benefits are enormous, but only if we use it effectively and responsibly. The potential for future innovations is huge, but we must focus on applying its power for positive impacts while minimizing risks.

The debate around AI and emotion management is complex. While there are valid concerns about giving machines control over our emotions and the potential for misuse, it's important to recognize AI's potential for good. AI, like any tool, can be used for both positive and negative purposes. It's up to us to ensure that we harness its power for the benefit of society.

By setting ethical guidelines and regulations, we can make sure that AI remains a tool that helps us, rather than something that controls us.

Chapter 7
Data Strategies in AI Marketing

Waking up in the morning. As you get out of bed, you notice the weather outside. *Is it sunny or rainy?* That's data. When you check your phone for the time, you're looking at more data. Data is all around us, and we collect it every day without even realizing it.

Data is just pieces of information. It can be anything from the number of steps you take in a day to your favorite song. We gather data from our experiences, conversations, and observations. For example, when you talk to your friend about a movie you both saw, you're sharing and collecting data about that movie.

Our brains are pretty good at remembering important information. You can recall your birthday, your best friend's name, and your home address because these pieces of data are significant to you. But there's a limit to how much we can remember. You might not recall what you ate for lunch two weeks ago because it's not as important.

The data we collect helps us make decisions. If you know it's going to rain, you bring an umbrella. If you remember that a certain food upset your stomach, you avoid eating it again. This personal data shapes our daily choices chand behaviors.

Does our data define us? In many ways, yes. The information we gather and remember reflects our interests and habits. If you love playing soccer, your data might include your favorite teams, players, and game statistics. This data shows what you care about and enjoy.

Data is just one part of who we are. While it tells a story about our preferences and actions, it doesn't capture everything. People are more than just the data they generate. Emotions, thoughts, and relationships also play a big role in defining us.

How Data Benefits Marketing for Businesses

Data is very important in modern marketing because it helps businesses make better decisions. By understanding their customers better, companies can improve how they market products, plan campaigns, and develop new items.

Data helps businesses know what their customers like and don't like. When companies look at what people have bought before, they can see which products are popular. This information lets them keep more of those products in stock, which makes customers happy and can increase sales. For example, Starbucks uses data from its loyalty program to see what drinks and snacks customers prefer. They then send special offers based on these preferences.

Data also allows businesses to personalize their marketing efforts. By knowing what a customer has bought or looked at before, companies can send them messages that match their interests. This makes the marketing more effective because it feels more personal. For instance, Amazon recommends products based on what you have previously viewed or purchased, making it more likely you'll find something you like.

Businesses can also use data to see how well their marketing campaigns are working. By tracking this in real-time, they can quickly see what is effective and what isn't, and make changes right away. This means they can spend their marketing money more wisely. Netflix, for example, uses data to understand viewing habits and recommend shows and movies that users are likely to enjoy, which keeps subscribers happy and engaged.

Data helps companies predict trends and stay ahead of the competition. By looking at data, businesses can spot trends and guess what customers will want in the future. This helps them prepare and stay competitive. Fashion retailers use data to predict what styles will be popular next season and stock their stores accordingly.

Improving the customer experience is another big benefit of data. By understanding how customers behave, companies can make their services better. For example, Uber uses data to optimize routes and reduce wait times, which makes the service more convenient for users.

Data guides product development. By analyzing feedback and how customers use products, companies can decide what features to add or change. Apple, for example, uses data from its devices to learn how customers use them, which helps in designing new features and products that meet customer needs.

Data Collection Techniques

AI plays an important role in gathering data from various sources, including social media, websites, and IoT devices. This process helps businesses collect valuable information that they can use to improve their products and services.

Social Media

Social media platforms like Facebook, Twitter, and Instagram are filled with data about people's preferences, opinions, and activities. AI tools can scan these platforms to collect data on what people are talking about. For instance, if many users are discussing a new smartphone, AI can gather this data to help businesses understand what features are attracting attention and what issues users are facing.

AI analyzes posts, comments, likes, and shares to determine trends and sentiments. This information helps businesses know what their customers like or dislike and how they can improve their products or services.

Websites

Websites track visitor behavior to understand how users interact with their content. AI helps in analyzing this data to provide insights about user interactions. When you visit a website, AI can track which pages you visit, how long you stay on each page, and what you click on.

An e-commerce website might use AI to see which products are being viewed the most, which ones are added to carts, and which ones are purchased. This helps businesses understand which products are popular and which ones might need more promotion or improvement.

IoT Devices

IoT (Internet of Things) devices are everyday objects connected to the Internet, such as smartwatches, home assistants, and even refrigerators. These devices collect data about their usage. AI analyzes this data to identify patterns and trends.

A smart thermostat collects data on temperature settings and adjustments throughout the day. AI can analyze this data to help energy companies understand usage patterns and optimize energy consumption. This can lead to recommendations for users on how to save energy and reduce costs.

Data from Multiple Sources

AI not only collects data from various sources but also integrates it to provide a comprehensive view. By combining data from social media, websites, and IoT devices, businesses can get a complete picture of customer behavior and preferences.

A Company might integrate data from social media mentions, website visits, and smart device usage to see if people who talk about their products online are also visiting their website and using their smart devices in specific ways. This integrated data helps businesses make better decisions and tailor their marketing strategies more effectively.

One of the significant advantages of AI is its ability to collect and analyze data in real time. This means businesses can get immediate insights into customer behavior and respond quickly. If a new product launch is receiving a lot of attention on social media, AI can alert the company, allowing it to quickly launch related marketing campaigns or address any emerging issues.

Data Management and Integration

Data management and integration are important for effective marketing strategies. AI helps businesses handle large amounts of data from various sources, ensuring consistency and accuracy.

Amazon Redshift

Amazon Redshift is a data warehouse service that allows businesses to collect, store, and analyze large amounts of data. It integrates data from various sources, making it easier to manage. A retail company can use Amazon Redshift to combine sales data from its website, social media, and in-store transactions. This unified data helps in understanding overall sales performance and customer preferences.

Google BigQuery

Google BigQuery is a cloud-based data warehouse that allows businesses to run fast SQL queries using the processing power of Google's infrastructure. It can handle large datasets and integrates data from multiple sources. An e-commerce business can use BigQuery to analyze data from its website, advertising campaigns, and customer feedback. This integrated data helps in making better marketing decisions based on comprehensive insights.

Snowflake

Snowflake is a cloud data platform that offers data storage, processing, and analytics solutions. It supports data integration from various sources, providing a single source of truth. A financial services company might use Snowflake to integrate data from its transaction systems, customer interactions, and market analysis tools. This integrated data helps in providing personalized financial advice and services to clients.

Benefits of AI-Driven Data Integration

Improved Decision-Making

AI-driven data integration provides a comprehensive view of customer behavior, helping businesses make better decisions. For example, by integrating data from social media, websites, and in-store interactions, a company can understand what products are popular and why. This insight helps in planning marketing strategies that target the right audience with the right message.

Enhanced Accuracy

AI tools ensure that data is accurate by eliminating duplicates and correcting errors. Accurate data is crucial for creating effective marketing strategies. For example, an AI tool can automatically update customer contact information from different sources, ensuring that the data is up-to-date and reliable.

Operational Efficiency

Managing and integrating data manually can be time-consuming and prone to errors. AI automates these processes, saving time and reducing the risk of mistakes. For instance, AI can continuously sync data from various marketing platforms, ensuring that all teams have access to the latest information without manual updates.

Example:

Nike, a global leader in sportswear, uses AI to manage and integrate data from various sources, enhancing customer experience and optimizing operations.

Nike is known for its innovative approach to sportswear and customer engagement. The brand leverages advanced technology to stay competitive and meet customer demands effectively.

Nike collects data from various touchpoints, including its websites, apps, and retail stores. For instance, the Nike Fit app uses AI and augmented reality to provide precise shoe-fitting recommendations by scanning customers' feet through their smartphone cameras. This ensures customers get the perfect fit, reducing returns and improving satisfaction.

Nike uses several AI tools and platforms to manage and integrate this data. The acquisition of companies like Invertex and Zodiac has enhanced Nike's ability to utilize AI for data analytics. Invertex's 3D scanning capabilities and Zodiac's predictive analytics help Nike understand customer preferences and predict future behaviors.

Benefits of AI Integration

- **Personalized Customer Experience:** AI helps Nike deliver a personalized shopping experience. By analyzing data from the Nike app, Nike Training Club, and other platforms, Nike can recommend products that match individual customer preferences. This personalized approach keeps customers engaged and satisfied.

- **Efficient Inventory Management:** AI tools like Celect optimize inventory by predicting future demand based on data analysis. This helps Nike maintain the right stock levels, reducing both overstock and stockouts, which enhances operational efficiency and meets customer demand more effectively.

- **Enhanced Decision-Making:** By integrating data from various sources, Nike gains comprehensive insights into market trends and customer behaviors. This data-driven approach enables Nike to make informed decisions about product development, marketing strategies, and customer engagement. Analyzing data from the Nike app helps Nike understand which products are popular and why, allowing them to focus their efforts on successful items.

- **Improved Customer Loyalty:** AI-driven insights enable Nike to offer personalized experiences and exclusive benefits through their NikePlus membership program. This strategy not only boosts revenue but also strengthens the emotional connection between Nike and its customers, fostering long-term loyalty.

Data-Driven Decision Making

Let's consider a company that sells home fitness equipment. They aim to increase sales of their new smart treadmill and use AI to guide their marketing decisions.

The company collects data from its website, mobile app, and customer feedback forms. AI tools help gather information about customer preferences, such as popular features and purchasing patterns.

AI analyzes the data to find patterns. It discovers that customers aged 25-45 are more interested in smart features like interactive workout programs and real-time performance tracking. The AI also identifies that these customers frequently use platforms like YouTube and Facebook for fitness content.

Based on this analysis, the company targets its marketing efforts towards the 25-45 age group. They create engaging video ads showcasing the smart treadmill's interactive features and post them on YouTube and Facebook. They also collaborate with fitness influencers who can demonstrate the treadmill's benefits.

AI continuously monitors the performance of these ads. It tracks metrics such as views, likes, shares, and conversion rates. The AI finds that videos highlighting personal success stories perform best. The company adjusts its content to include more testimonials and real-life usage scenarios.

Using AI to guide their marketing decisions, the company sees a significant increase in sales of their new smart treadmill. Customer engagement on YouTube and Facebook rises, and the brand gains more visibility in the fitness community. The AI-driven strategy ensures that marketing efforts are effective and resonate with the target audience.

Data is Everything

Think about this book. It's a collection of data organized to give you insights into AI and marketing. As you finish this chapter, ask yourself: *What will you remember? What stood out to you?*

Just like you're processing this information, businesses use data to understand their customers. Data is everywhere, shaping decisions and driving success. *Will this chapter's insights stay with you?* Time will tell, but one thing is clear: data is at the core of everything we do.

Chapter 8
Virtual Influencers and Brand Strategy

Influencers can make a huge difference for a business, especially when it comes to gaining traction and visibility. When a well-known influencer promotes a product, it can reach a vast audience almost instantly. This can be particularly powerful for new brands looking to make their mark.

Influencers build trust with their followers. People follow them because they relate to them and trust their recommendations. When an influencer talks about a product, it feels like a recommendation from a good friend. This trust can lead to more people trying out the product, which in turn can boost sales and brand awareness.

The reach of influencers is another big advantage. They can introduce a product to a large and diverse audience. For instance, a single post from a popular Instagram influencer can be seen by hundreds of thousands of people worldwide. This kind of exposure is invaluable for any brand.

Influencers also create engaging content around the products they promote. They post photos, videos, and stories that show the product in use. This promotes the product and provides the brand with high-quality content that can be used on its own social media channels.

The interactive nature of social media means that influencer campaigns often drive significant engagement. Followers comment, like, share, and sometimes create their own content in response to an influencer's post. This buzz creates a sense of community around the brand and encourages more people to check out the product.

One of the great things about influencer marketing is that it offers measurable results. Brands can track likes, shares, comments, and, most importantly, sales. This data helps brands see exactly how much impact an influencer campaign is having and allows them to adjust their strategies accordingly.

Daniel Wellington (DW) is a great example of how a brand can achieve massive success through influencer marketing. Founded in 2011, DW's watches were not luxury items, but they gained a lot of traction due to a very effective strategy that focused on working with influencers. Rather than investing large sums in traditional advertising, DW sent their watches to thousands of influencers, from micro-influencers to bigger names like Hailey Bieber, Selena Gomez, and Korean actor Lee Jong Suk.

This simple approach—giving watches to influencers in exchange for social media posts—led to an explosion of content featuring their products. In fact, by 2019, Daniel Wellington was the most frequently mentioned watch brand on Instagram, with the hashtag #danielwellington generating over 166 million views on TikTok and more than 2.4 million posts on Instagram. Scrolling through even just the most recent posts takes minutes of non-stop scrolling.

One particularly clever part of DW's strategy was encouraging user-generated content (UGC) by offering influencers personalized promo codes. This allowed them to track the effectiveness of each influencer's campaign while giving their audience an incentive to purchase. This use of UGC, paired with influencer collaborations, helped DW grow from a small startup into a globally recognized brand with more than $200 million in revenue.

The Rise of Virtual Influencers: Brands Creating AI-Generated Personas

Virtual influencers, or AI-generated personas, have become a significant trend in the marketing world. These are computer-generated with meticulously crafted personalities, engaging audiences and revolutionizing the world of marketing. Like real influencers, they also have their own interests, dislikes, stories, and social networks. These digital entities are designed to engage with audiences in ways that human influencers do but with added benefits and some unique challenges.

How Do Virtual Influencers Operate?

Virtual influencers, as opposed to real ones, are totally under the direction of the companies, organizations, or people that created them. More control over messaging and brand alignment is made possible by this. Like their real-world counterparts, they engage with brands, promote goods, share content, and take part in social issues.

- **Lil Miquela:** One of the most well-known virtual influencers, Lil Miquela, created by the startup Brud, has millions of followers across Instagram and TikTok. She has collaborated with top fashion brands like Prada, Dior, and Calvin Klein, and even released music, showing how versatile and impactful a virtual influencer can be in various marketing domains.

- **Lu do Magalu**: Created by the Brazilian retail giant Magazine Luiza, Lu do Magalu is the most followed virtual influencer globally. She engages audiences with lifestyle content and product reviews, seamlessly integrating with the brand's marketing strategies. Her presence has helped the company reach a wider audience and enhance brand engagement.

- **Thalasya**: Developed by Magnavem Studio, Thalasya is an AI influencer from Indonesia who explores various locales, promoting hotels, restaurants, and even health products. She has over 460,000 followers on Instagram and has her own clothing store, showcasing her versatility in promoting diverse products and services.

Advantages and Challenges of Virtual Influencers

Advantages

Virtual influencers offer several significant benefits for brands:

- **Always Available**: Virtual influencers are available 24/7. They don't need breaks, vacations, or sleep, making them ideal for continuous engagement with a global audience. This constant availability ensures that followers can interact with the influencer at any time, which can be especially beneficial for international campaigns.

- **Total Control**: Brands have complete control over a virtual influencer's persona, behavior, and messaging. This means the influencer always stays on-brand, and there is no risk of scandals or off-script moments that human influencers might have. This level of control allows for a consistent and reliable marketing strategy, ensuring that the influencer's behavior aligns perfectly with the brand's values.

- **Cost-Effective in the Long Run**: Although the initial development of a virtual influencer can be costly, they don't require ongoing salaries, travel expenses, or other perks that human influencers do. Over time, this can lead to significant cost savings for the brand, making virtual influencers a cost-effective solution in the long run.

- **Highly Adaptable**: Virtual influencers can be tailored to fit various campaigns and brand strategies. They can easily switch roles, adopt new personas, and appear in multiple campaigns simultaneously without any scheduling conflicts. This adaptability makes them versatile marketing tools, capable of adjusting to different marketing needs and trends.

Challenges

However, using virtual influencers also comes with several challenges:

- **Public Acceptance**: Some audiences may be skeptical about interacting with virtual influencers, finding it hard to trust recommendations from a digital persona. This skepticism can impact the effectiveness of marketing campaigns. Brands need to work on building credibility and trust with their audience when using virtual influencers.

- **Authenticity Issues**: Virtual influencers might lack the genuine human touch that audiences look for. Followers might question the authenticity of endorsements and whether the influencer truly uses or believes in the products they promote. Ensuring transparency about the virtual nature of these influencers is crucial to maintaining trust.

- **Ethical Considerations**: There are significant ethical concerns, such as promoting unrealistic beauty standards and potential biases in AI-generated content. Brands must navigate these issues carefully to maintain trust and credibility with their audience. Addressing these concerns openly and responsibly is essential for ethical marketing.

- **High Initial Costs and Maintenance**: Creating a sophisticated virtual influencer requires a substantial initial investment in technology and design. Additionally, ongoing maintenance and updates are necessary to keep the influencer relevant and engaging, which can add to the costs. Despite the potential cost savings in the long run, the initial investment can be a barrier for some brands.

Case Studies: Examples of Brands That Have Successfully Integrated Virtual Influencers

Imma and IKEA

IKEA partnered with Imma, a virtual influencer created by the Japanese company Aww Inc. Imma is known for her pink bob and digital persona, and she has over 390,000 followers on Instagram. IKEA used Imma to show off their furniture and home accessories in a series of eye-catching posts. The campaign featured Imma living in a storefront apartment in Harajuku for three days, interacting with IKEA products, and showing how they can be used in daily life. This helped IKEA connect with a tech-savvy audience and highlighted the blend of lifestyle and virtual technology.

Janky and 7-Eleven

Janky, a virtual cat created by Superplastic, teamed up with 7-Eleven to promote their brand. Janky has a playful and quirky personality, and he engages with 7-Eleven's products in fun ways. The campaign included social media posts and videos where Janky interacted with various 7-Eleven items, generating a lot of interest from younger audiences. This partnership showed how a fun virtual character can boost brand visibility and connect with a digital-native crowd.

FN Meka and Capitol Records

FN Meka is an AI-generated virtual rapper with millions of followers on TikTok and Instagram. He made headlines when Capitol Records signed him, making him the first AI artist to get a major label deal. FN Meka's music and persona are completely AI-generated, and his digital presence has attracted a large following. Capitol Records used FN Meka to explore new ways of marketing music, engaging audiences with fresh content, and expanding their reach in the digital space.

Shudu and Balmain

Shudu, often called the world's first digital supermodel, worked with luxury fashion brand Balmain. Created by digital artist Cameron-James Wilson, Shudu has modeled for several high-end brands, bringing a futuristic edge to their campaigns. Balmain's campaign with Shudu was well-received, showing how virtual influencers can effectively represent luxury brands and appeal to fashion-forward consumers. Shudu's realistic and captivating presence helped Balmain reach a wider audience and strengthen its innovative brand image.

Understanding these real-world applications can help brands plan their own strategies with virtual influencers. The symbiotic relationship between virtual influencers and companies is evidence of the revolutionary potential of technology in influencing the evolution of marketing and communication in the future. Finding the right virtual persona that matches the brand's values and connects with the target audience is key to a successful campaign.

Chapter 9
Generative AI and Marketing Innovation

Generative AI is a form of artificial intelligence that can produce new content. It can write text, create images, compose music, and design products.

For businesses, generative AI offers a range of exciting possibilities. Imagine having an AI that can write engaging blog posts, and **social media content,** create eye-catching marketing graphics, or even design custom products based on customer preferences. This can save time and resources, allowing your team to focus on other important tasks.

But how exactly can generative AI benefit your company? Okay Let's begin with an example,

To the World,

We are beyond excited to introduce you to Kalakriti Shoes! Imagine combining the spirit of art with the comfort of your favorite sneakers—that's what we're all about. Our journey started with a dream to create unique, hand-painted canvas shoes that add a splash of personality to your every step.

At Kalakriti, each shoe is a masterpiece, meticulously painted by talented local artists from all corners of India. Every brushstroke tells a story, and no two pairs are the same. Whether you're into bold, vibrant designs or something more understated, we've got something that'll catch your eye.

We know what you're thinking—why hand-painted shoes? Because we believe in celebrating individuality. Our shoes are not just footwear; they're an expression of who you are. And the best part? You'll never have that awkward moment of wearing the same shoes as someone else at a party!

Our shoes are for everyone, from fashion-forward men and women to those who just want a little extra flair in their wardrobe. They're comfortable, stylish, and made with love.

By choosing Kalakriti Shoes, you're supporting a community of artists and helping to keep the beautiful tradition of hand painting alive. We're all about fair trade, ensuring our artists are paid fairly for their incredible work. Your support makes a real difference in their lives.

We invite you to step into the world of Kalakriti Shoes. Wear our art, tell your story, and stand out from the crowd. Check out our collection on our website and find the perfect pair that speaks to you.

Thank you for joining us on this colorful adventure. We can't wait to see where your Kalakriti Shoes take you!

Warm regards,

The Kalakriti Shoes Team

P.S. Follow us on social media for updates on new designs, behind-the-scenes peeks, and special offers. We'd love to connect with you!

First Social Media Post

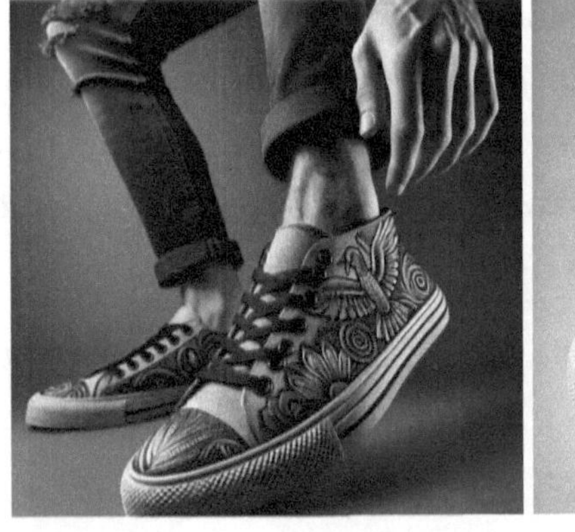

(Image from Mid-Journey AI)

Caption:

✨ Welcome to Kalakriti Shoes! ✨

We're thrilled to introduce our unique hand-painted designer canvas shoes, crafted with love by talented local artists. Each pair is a masterpiece, perfect for adding a splash of creativity to your everyday style.

👟 Our first collection is here, and we have an exclusive offer for you! Enjoy a 10% discount on your first purchase with the code

FIRSTSTEP

🖌 Step into comfort and art with Kalakriti Shoes. Visit our website to explore our collection and find your perfect pair.

📷 Shot with Canon 5D, 35mm Signature Prime Lens

#KalakritiShoes #HandPaintedShoes #WearableArt #Support LocalArtists #FashionWithAPurpose

Additional Tags

#NewArrivals#UniqueStyle#FashionArt#ComfortAndStyle#Sustain ableFashion#MadeInIndia#ArtisticFootwear#FirstPurchaseDiscount #ExclusiveOffer

Ad Script: "Kalakriti Shoes - The New Street Style Revolution"

[Opening Shot] *Scene: A crowded street in Mumbai with a group of young people hanging out, laughing, and having a good time. Quick cuts to similar scenes in New York, Tokyo, and Paris.*

[Voiceover] (Exciting, energetic tone) "From Mumbai to New York, Tokyo to Paris, the streets are alive with a new kind of energy."

[Cut to Close-Up] *Scene: Close-up of a pair of Kalakriti Shoes being laced up, showcasing the vibrant hand-painted designs.*

[Voiceover] (Confident, engaging tone) "Introducing Kalakriti Shoes – where art meets the street."

[Cut to Action Shots] *Scene: People wearing Kalakriti Shoes skateboarding, dancing, walking through graffiti-covered alleys, and attending street festivals.*

[Voiceover] (Upbeat, dynamic tone) "These aren't just shoes; they're a canvas for your creativity, a statement of your individuality."

[Cut to Different Shots] *Scene: Close-up shots of different Kalakriti Shoe designs, highlighting the intricate details and vibrant colors.*

[Voiceover] (Creative, inspiring tone) "Hand-painted by local artists, each pair is a unique masterpiece."

[Cut to Montage] *Scene: Quick cuts of people from different cultures and backgrounds all wearing Kalakriti Shoes, showcasing the global appeal.*

[Voiceover] (Inclusive, universal tone) "Made for everyone, designed for you."

[Cut to Shot of a Person Walking Down a Street] *Scene: A person walks confidently down a busy street, wearing Kalakriti Shoes, turning heads as they go.*

[Voiceover] (Motivational, compelling tone) "Step into the future of street style."

[End Shot] *Scene: The Kalakriti Shoes logo appears on the screen with the tagline "Hand-Painted Designer Canvas".*

[Voiceover] (Closing with a call-to-action) "Get your pair now at KalakritiShoes.com. Join the revolution. Wear your art."

[Additional Text on Screen] "Follow us @KalakritiShoes for the latest designs and exclusive offers."

[Music Fades Out]

Generative AI Prompt for Jingle Creation

Energetic and Vibrant Jingle for Kalakriti Shoes Ad. Create a custom music track for an advertisement promoting Kalakriti Shoes, a brand of hand-painted designer canvas shoes. The jingle should be energetic, vibrant, and catchy to reflect the artistic and dynamic nature of the brand. The music should evoke a sense of creativity, fun, and individuality, appealing to a diverse and global audience.

Upbeat Pop with elements of Electronic Dance Music (EDM). The mood is energetic, inspiring, and uplifting with a fast-paced tempo. The instrumentation includes bright synths, rhythmic drums, catchy basslines, and occasional guitar riffs, lasting for 30-45 seconds. The structure features a strong, catchy intro, a vibrant and energetic chorus, a slight dip in intensity to highlight the tagline, and ends on a high note with the chorus.

The music is designed to complement visuals of young, diverse individuals confidently wearing Kalakriti Shoes in various urban settings. It aims to be memorable, and capable of lingering in the audience's mind long after they've seen the ad.

Use this prompt with a generative AI tool like Amper Music, or Suno AI to create the perfect jingle for your advertisement.

SEO Plan for Kalakriti Shoes

Launching Kalakriti Shoes into the digital space requires a solid SEO strategy to ensure we reach our **right** target audience effectively. Here's a detailed and structured plan to enhance our online visibility, drive organic traffic, and boost our search engine rankings.

Keyword Research

First, we need to identify the key terms our potential customers are searching for. We'll use tools like Google Keyword Planner, Ahrefs, and SEMrush to find relevant keywords.

1. **Primary Keywords:** Our main focus will be on terms like "hand-painted shoes," "designer canvas shoes," and "artistic footwear."

2. **Secondary Keywords:** We'll also target phrases like "hand-painted designer canvas shoes," "Indian handcrafted shoes," and "unique street style footwear."

3. **Long-Tail Keywords:** To capture more specific searches, we'll use long-tail keywords such as "where to buy hand-painted shoes," "best custom canvas shoes," and "artistic footwear for street style."

On-Page SEO

Our website needs to be optimized for these keywords to ensure that search engines can easily find and rank our pages.

- **Title Tags:** Each page will have a unique and descriptive title tag that includes our primary keywords.

- **Meta Descriptions:** We'll write compelling meta descriptions with our primary and secondary keywords, keeping them under 160 characters.

- **Headings:** We'll use H1 tags for main titles and H2/H3 for subheadings, naturally incorporating keywords.

- **URL Structure:** Clean, keyword-rich URLs will help, such as "kalakritishoes.com/hand-painted-canvas-shoes."

- **Content Optimization:** High-quality, original content is key. We'll weave primary, secondary, and long-tail keywords naturally into our text, without keyword stuffing.

- **Image Optimization:** High-quality images with descriptive file names and alt text will improve visibility. For example, an image might be named "hand-painted-shoe.jpg."

- **Mobile Optimization:** Ensuring our site is mobile-friendly is crucial, as many users will visit from their phones.

Content Strategy

Creating valuable and engaging content will help us attract and retain customers.

- **Blog Posts:** Regular posts on topics like "The Art of Hand-Painted Shoes" or "How to Style Canvas Shoes" will draw in readers and keep them engaged.

- **Guest Blogging:** Writing guest posts for popular fashion and lifestyle blogs can build backlinks and increase brand awareness.

- **Product Descriptions:** Detailed, keyword-rich descriptions for each product will highlight their unique features and craftsmanship.

- **Social Media Integration:** Sharing blog posts, product updates, and customer reviews on social media platforms will drive traffic to our website.

Technical SEO

Technical aspects of SEO ensure that our site runs smoothly and is easily accessible by search engines.

- **Site Speed:** Optimizing images and using a content delivery network (CDN) will help improve site speed.

- **Sitemap:** Creating and submitting an XML sitemap to Google Search Console will aid in indexing our pages.

- **Robots.txt:** Correctly configuring the robots.txt file will guide search engine crawlers.

- **SSL Certificate:** Ensuring our website has an SSL certificate will secure user data and improve trust.

- **Structured Data:** Using schema markup will help search engines understand our content better and improve our visibility in search results.

Off-Page SEO

Building our online presence beyond our website is crucial for attracting more visitors.

- **Backlink Building:** We'll reach out to fashion bloggers, influencers, and industry websites for backlinks. Creating shareable content like infographics and videos will also encourage natural backlinking.

- **Social Media Presence:** Actively engaging with followers on social media and using ads to promote new products and blog posts will drive traffic to our site.

- **Online Directories:** Listing Kalakriti Shoes in online business directories and fashion-related directories will enhance our online presence.

Local SEO

Optimizing for local searches will help us attract nearby customers.

- **Google My Business:** Creating and optimizing a Google My Business profile with accurate information, photos, and customer reviews will enhance our local visibility.

- **Local Listings:** Ensuring our business is listed in local directories and on maps with consistent name, address, and phone number (NAP) information is crucial.

- **Localized Content:** Creating content that targets local keywords and trends, like "best hand-painted shoes in Mumbai," will draw in local customers.

Monitoring and Analytics

Regularly tracking and analyzing our performance will help us adjust our strategy as needed.

- **Key Metrics:** We'll monitor organic traffic, keyword rankings, bounce rate, conversion rate, and backlinks.

- **Regular Audits:** Conducting regular SEO audits will help identify and fix issues. We'll also monitor keyword performance and adjust our strategies based on the data.

Article 1: Discover the Magic of Kalakriti Shoes

Hello everyone!

We are thrilled to introduce you to Kalakriti Shoes, where each pair of shoes is a canvas of art and creativity. Our journey began with a simple idea: to bring together the beauty of hand-painted designs and the comfort of canvas shoes. And now, we are excited to share this with you.

Hand-Painted with Love

At Kalakriti Shoes, we believe in celebrating individuality and creativity. Every pair of our shoes is hand-painted by talented local artists. This means that each shoe is unique, just like you. Whether you prefer vibrant, eye-catching designs or subtle, elegant patterns, we have something that will match your style perfectly.

We know that comfort is key when it comes to footwear. That's why we use high-quality canvas that is both durable and breathable. Our shoes are designed to keep your feet comfortable all day long, whether you're strolling through the city or hanging out with friends.

When you buy Kalakriti Shoes, you're not just getting a pair of shoes; you're supporting a community of local artists. We are committed to fair trade and ensuring our artists are compensated fairly for their amazing work. Your purchase helps sustain their craft and supports their livelihoods.

We invite you to explore our collection and find the pair of shoes that speak to you. Each pair tells a story and is a testament to the artistry and dedication of our team. Visit our website to see the full range of designs and join the Kalakriti family.

Thank you for supporting Kalakriti Shoes. We can't wait to see you step out in style and comfort.

Warm regards,
The Kalakriti Shoes Team

Article 2: Step into Art with Kalakriti Shoes

Hey there!

Welcome to Kalakriti Shoes, where every step you take is a step into art. Our shoes are not just footwear; they are a celebration of creativity, comfort, and style. We are excited to share our passion for hand-painted shoes with you.

Each pair of Kalakriti Shoes is hand-painted by skilled local artists. This means that no two pairs are the same. Our artists pour their hearts into creating designs that are as unique as the people who wear them. Whether you're looking for something bold and colorful or something more understated, you'll find it here.

Our shoes are made from high-quality canvas, which makes them both comfortable and durable. We believe that style should never come at the expense of comfort, and with Kalakriti Shoes, you get the best of both worlds. Perfect for a day out or a casual evening, our shoes are designed to keep you comfortable.

By choosing Kalakriti Shoes, you're supporting local artists and their incredible work. We believe in fair trade and ensuring our artists are paid fairly for their talent and hard work. Your purchase helps sustain their craft and brings their beautiful designs to life.

We invite you to explore our collection of hand-painted shoes. Each pair tells a story and is a testament to the artistry and dedication of our team. Visit our website to find your perfect pair and join the Kalakriti community.

Thank you for being a part of our journey. We can't wait to see you step into art with Kalakriti Shoes.

Best wishes,

The Kalakriti Shoes Team

Everything you've seen here, from the logo to the introduction articles, was created using generative AI. This amazing technology helped design the Kalakriti Shoes logo, craft engaging introduction articles, create the first social media post, and even come up with a compelling ad script. It also helped generate a prompt for creating a jingle, develop a detailed SEO plan, and write informative marketing articles.

Having all your marketing materials ready in a fraction of the time it would usually take. That's the power of generative AI. It's not just about creating content; it's about creating smart, effective, and engaging content that can help your business grow.

While exploring Kalakriti Shoes, note that all materials were generated by AI. This showcases AI's ability to revolutionize marketing, enhancing its efficiency.

Generative AI in Marketing

Generative AI is transforming how marketing works. It's a smart tool that creates interesting content based on what customers like and say. What makes it special is its ability to change quickly in response to customer feedback. This means marketers can adjust their messages in real time, making their campaigns more effective and relevant.

Think about being able to change your marketing message instantly based on what customers are doing and saying. That's what generative AI can do. It looks at data from social media, customer reviews, and buying habits to create content that really connects with people. This keeps marketing fresh and in tune with the audience.

Generative AI isn't just about doing things automatically. It's about making a real connection with customers. For example, it can create personalized emails, social media posts, and even unique visuals that match what the brand stands for and what the audience likes.

The great thing about generative AI is how flexible and creative it is. It can make all kinds of content, from text to images to videos, all designed to catch the audience's eye. And because it learns over time, the content it creates keeps getting better and better, becoming more aligned with what customers want.

Showrunner Platform

One of the most innovative uses of generative AI in marketing comes from Fable Studio with its platform, Showrunner. This platform is breaking new ground by allowing users to create AI-powered animated TV shows, uniquely blending entertainment and technology.

Fable Studio's Showrunner platform democratizes content creation, making it accessible to anyone, not just professional filmmakers. Users can describe the type of show they want, and within minutes, the AI generates an animated series based on their input. This interactive approach means viewers are no longer passive consumers but active participants in the creative process.

Showrunner's notable project, "Exit Valley," is a satirical series that takes a humorous look at Silicon Valley. The show runs on Sim Francisco, a detailed simulation of the tech hub. Users can upload themselves, friends, and characters into the simulation to create personalized content. This feature makes the content more engaging and allows for a high degree of personalization and relatability.

The platform has already attracted significant interest, with a waitlist of 50,000 users eager to try it out. Showrunner is currently offering an Alpha program for early adopters, giving them a chance to be part of this pioneering experience.

Showrunner's ability to blur the lines between viewer and creator opens up new possibilities for content creation and marketing. It exemplifies how generative AI can create innovative marketing campaigns that are creative, engaging, highly personalized, and interactive.

Generative Tools in Action

Generative AI tools are changing how content is created and designed. They let users generate text, images, music, and more with just a few prompts. Check out some top generative AI tools below:

ChatGPT (OpenAI)

ChatGPT is an advanced language model created by OpenAI that generates human-like text based on the prompts it receives. It's designed to carry on conversations, answer questions, write essays, and much more. Let's delve into how ChatGPT is being used in marketing, its advantages, and how it compares to other generative AI tools.

Description: ChatGPT is a powerful tool that can produce coherent and contextually relevant text. This ability makes it highly versatile, allowing it to be used in a wide range of applications from casual conversation to professional content creation. It understands and generates natural language, making it feel like you're interacting with a human.

Usage in Marketing: In the world of marketing, ChatGPT shines brightly. Marketers can leverage this tool to quickly create engaging content such as blog posts, social media updates, and email newsletters. It's great for brainstorming ideas, generating marketing copy, and drafting responses to customer inquiries. Imagine needing fresh content for a blog post or an eye-catching caption for a social media post—ChatGPT can handle it all efficiently. Its ability to understand context and produce relevant text helps in maintaining a consistent brand voice, ensuring that all communication resonates well with the target audience.

Advantages: One of the main advantages of ChatGPT is its ability to generate text that is both coherent and contextually appropriate. It can tailor content to different audiences, making sure the messaging hits the right notes. This is particularly useful for marketers who need to create personalized content for various segments of their audience. Additionally, ChatGPT can handle a large volume of content generation, making it an efficient tool for scaling marketing efforts. It saves time and effort, allowing marketers to focus on strategy and creative direction.

Standing Out Among Other Tools: What sets ChatGPT apart from other generative AI tools is its conversational ability. While tools like DALL-E excel in creating images and others like MidJourney focus on artistic visuals, ChatGPT's strength lies in its next-generation capabilities. It can engage in detailed dialogues, which is ideal for customer service chatbots and interactive marketing campaigns. Its human-like understanding and generation of text make it perfect for creating personalized marketing experiences. Whether it's crafting a tailored email to a specific customer or engaging in real-time conversations, ChatGPT provides a level of interaction that is highly valuable in marketing.

DALL-E (OpenAI): DALL-E creates images from textual descriptions. This tool can produce detailed and imaginative visuals perfect for marketing, entertainment, and design. Marketers can use DALL-E to create custom illustrations for ads or social media posts, ensuring that visuals match their brand message. For instance, if a brand wants an image of a cat in a space suit, DALL-E can generate that specific visual.

MidJourney: MidJourney is known for generating high-quality, artistic images from text prompts. It's popular among artists, designers, and marketers for creating visually striking images. For example, an apparel brand can use MidJourney to produce vibrant images for its seasonal campaigns, catching the audience's eye with unique visuals.

Stable Diffusion: Stable Diffusion is an open-source tool that generates detailed images based on text inputs. It's widely used in graphic design, advertising, and digital art. Digital artists and advertisers use Stable Diffusion to create compelling visuals for promotional materials and product launches. Its capability to produce intricate images makes it a valuable tool for visual content creation.

Gemini: Previously known as Google Bard. Gemini is a generative AI tool from Google that creates text and poetry based on prompts. It leverages Google's advanced language models to generate engaging content. Content creators can use Gemini to craft catchy slogans, engaging blog posts, and creative copy for marketing campaigns. Its creativity makes it a useful tool for generating unique and memorable content.

GitHub Copilot: GitHub Copilot is an AI-powered code completion tool that helps developers write code faster by suggesting lines or blocks of code. This tool is invaluable for software developers looking to increase productivity and reduce coding time. Developers working on a website for a marketing campaign can use Copilot to speed up the coding process, ensuring a faster launch.

RunwayML: RunwayML offers a suite of AI tools for creatives, including models for generating images, videos, and 3D content. It's used in video production, animation, and digital art to create innovative effects. Video producers can use RunwayML to create stunning visual effects for commercials and promotional videos.

Suno AI: Suno AI specializes in generating realistic audio and music through AI. It can create original soundtracks, sound effects, and voiceovers. Advertisers can use Suno AI to create captivating background music and sound effects for their commercials. Its ability to produce high-quality audio content enhances the impact of marketing campaigns.

Jasper AI: Jasper AI is a writing assistant that helps create content for blogs, social media, and marketing materials. It generates text that matches the user's style and tone, streamlining the writing process and enhancing content quality. A small business can use Jasper AI to create engaging social media posts and blog articles, maintaining a consistent brand voice.

DeepDream Generator: DeepDream Generator is an image manipulation tool that uses neural networks to create dream-like visuals from existing images. It's popular among artists and designers for creating unique artwork. Designers can use DeepDream Generator to produce surreal visuals for marketing campaigns, adding a distinctive touch to their projects.

Adobe Firefly: Adobe Firefly is a generative AI tool in Adobe Creative Cloud. It helps create vector graphics, images, and videos through AI, making it powerful for designers and marketers. Marketers can use Firefly to create stunning graphics and animations for their digital marketing campaigns. Its integration with Adobe's tools enhances the creative workflow.

Fotor: Fotor is an online photo editing tool that uses AI to enhance images, apply effects, and create designs. It's used by photographers and social media influencers to improve image quality and create visually appealing posts. Influencers can use Fotor to enhance their photos and create engaging social media content.

Artbreeder: Artbreeder is a collaborative tool that uses AI to generate and evolve images. Users can mix different images to create unique visuals, useful for character design, concept art, and visual storytelling. Game developers can use Artbreeder to create unique character designs and concept art for their games.

This Person Does Not Exist: This tool generates realistic images of non-existent people using AI. Each refresh creates a new, unique face. It's used in game development, virtual environments, and for creating avatars without models. Developers can use this tool to generate realistic avatars for virtual reality applications.

WriteSonic: WriteSonic is an AI writing tool that generates marketing copy, blog posts, and other content. It reduces the time spent on writing tasks while maintaining high-quality outputs. Marketing teams can use WriteSonic to generate persuasive copy for ads, landing pages, and email campaigns, ensuring effective and engaging content.

Framework for Using Generative AI in Marketing

TAG Framework

T - Task

Define the Specific Job or Activity

- Clearly state what you want the AI to do.

- Example: Create a marketing campaign for a new organic coffee brand.

A - Action

Describe How the AI Should Approach the Task

- Specify how the AI should carry out the task.

- Example: Use friendly and engaging language to write social media posts, and generate eye-catching images that highlight the coffee's natural ingredients.

G - Goal

Outline the Desired Outcome or Purpose

- Describe the expected results of the AI's work.

- Example: Increase social media engagement and drive traffic to the coffee brand's website.

RACE Framework

R - Role

Define the Role the AI Will Play

- Clarify what part the AI will take in the task.

- Example: AI will generate content for social media posts.

A - Action

Specify the Actions the AI Will Take

- Detail what actions the AI should perform.

- Example: Write engaging captions and create visuals for Instagram and Facebook.

C - Context

Provide Background Information and Context

- Give the AI the necessary background to understand the task.

- Example: The coffee brand is eco-friendly, and the target audience is health-conscious millennials.

E - Expectation

Set Clear Expectations for the Outcome

- Explain what you expect to achieve.

- Example: Expect an increase in social media followers and higher engagement rates.

Sample Prompts Using TAG Framework

Prompt 1: Social Media Campaign for Organic Coffee

Task: Create a marketing campaign for an organic coffee brand.

Action: Write engaging social media posts using friendly and approachable language. Generate eye-catching images of the coffee with vibrant backgrounds.

Goal: Promote the new product launch on social media, aiming to increase brand awareness and drive website traffic.

Output

Post 1:

- **Caption:** "🌱 Sip sustainably with our new organic coffee blend! Bursting with rich flavors and ethically sourced ingredients, every cup supports our planet. 🌍 ✨ #OrganicCoffee #EcoFriendly #CoffeeLovers"

- **Image:** A vibrant image of a steaming cup of coffee on a rustic wooden table, surrounded by fresh coffee beans and green leaves.

Post 2:

- **Caption:** "Start your day with a boost of natural goodness! Our organic coffee is not only delicious but also kind to the environment. 🍃 ☕ #MorningRitual #SustainableLiving #DrinkBetter"

- **Image:** A cozy morning scene with a cup of coffee, a newspaper, and a small plant on a sunny kitchen table.

Post 3:

- **Caption:** "Good coffee, great planet! Enjoy the bold taste of our new organic blend, knowing you're making a difference. 🌍 💚 #CoffeeWithACause #EthicalSourcing #GreenLiving"

- **Image:** An outdoor shot of a person enjoying coffee in a garden, with vibrant flowers and greenery in the background.

Post 4:

- **Caption:** "Discover the taste of nature with our organic coffee. Perfect for those who care about quality and sustainability. ☕ 🌿 #OrganicLife #QualityCoffee #EcoConscious"

- **Image:** A close-up of a coffee cup with latte art, placed next to a bag of organic coffee beans and a small chalkboard sign that says "100% Organic."

Post 5:

- **Caption:** "Join the organic revolution! Our new blend is here to redefine your coffee experience with pure, natural flavors. 🌱 ☕ #NewBlend #OrganicGoodness #CoffeeTime"

- **Image:** A vibrant, colorful flat lay of a coffee setup with various coffee-making tools, beans, and a cup of freshly brewed coffee.

Prompt 2: Launch Event Announcement

Task: Announce a virtual launch event for the new coffee product.

Action: Write a detailed post explaining the event, including the date, time, and special features. Create an attractive event banner.

Goal: Increase sign-ups and attendance for the launch event.

Output

Caption: "🎉 Join us for the virtual launch of our new organic coffee blend! ☕🌱 Discover the rich flavors and sustainable practices behind our latest creation.

📅 Date: September 20, 2024

🕐 Time: 7 PM EST

🎁 Special Features: Live coffee tasting, Q&A with our head roaster, and exclusive discounts for attendees!

Don't miss out—RSVP today and be a part of this exciting event! #CoffeeLaunch #VirtualEvent #OrganicCoffee"

Image: A beautifully designed event banner featuring a coffee cup with steam art, the event details prominently displayed, and a background of lush coffee plants.

Sample Prompts Using RACE Framework

Prompt 1: Instagram Post for New Coffee Blend

Role: AI will generate content for an Instagram post.

Action: Write a caption that highlights the new blend's unique flavors and benefits. Create a visual featuring the coffee blend with vibrant, engaging elements.

Context: The coffee brand focuses on organic and eco-friendly products. The target audience is young adults who are coffee enthusiasts.

Expectation: Increase engagement and attract new followers.

Output

Caption: "Experience the pure, bold flavors of our new organic coffee blend! ☕ Crafted with care for the environment and your taste buds. Perfect for your daily coffee ritual. #NewBlend #OrganicCoffee #EcoFriendly"

Image: A bright and engaging photo of the new coffee blend packaging with a steaming cup of coffee, placed on a table with a few coffee beans scattered around.

Prompt 2: Blog Post on Sustainable Coffee Farming

Role: AI will write a blog post.

Action: Write a detailed blog post explaining the process and benefits of sustainable coffee farming.

Context: The coffee brand supports sustainable farming practices. The target audience includes environmentally conscious consumers.

Expectation: Educate readers and enhance the brand's reputation as an eco-friendly company.

Output:

Title: "The Journey of Sustainable Coffee Farming: From Bean to Cup"

Introduction

Sustainable coffee farming is more than just a trend—it's a commitment to preserving our planet and supporting coffee-growing communities. In this post, we explore the journey of sustainable coffee farming and its many benefits.

- **What is Sustainable Coffee Farming?**

  Sustainable coffee farming involves practices that protect the environment, support fair labor, and promote economic stability for farmers. This includes organic farming, shade-grown coffee, and fair trade practices.

Benefits of Sustainable Coffee Farming

- **Environmental Protection:** Sustainable practices reduce deforestation, conserve water, and promote biodiversity.

- **Quality Coffee:** Organic methods produce coffee with rich, authentic flavors.

- **Support for Farmers:** Fairtrade ensures farmers receive fair compensation, improving their quality of life.

- **Our Commitment to Sustainability:**

  At [Your Coffee Brand], we are dedicated to sustainable farming practices. Our new organic blend is sourced from farms that prioritize environmental and social responsibility.

By choosing sustainable coffee, you're supporting a healthier planet and better livelihoods for farmers. Enjoy your cup of coffee knowing that it makes a positive impact.

Image: An image of a coffee farm with lush greenery and workers picking coffee cherries, showcasing the natural beauty of sustainable farming.

This framework, along with the prompts and outputs, offers a clear and effective way to use generative AI in marketing. By using the TAG and RACE frameworks, you can make sure your AI-based marketing is focused, engaging, and successful.

How Generative AI Benefits Marketing Campaigns

Generative AI offers significant advantages for marketing campaigns, transforming traditional strategies into more dynamic and effective efforts.

Personalization

Generative AI excels at creating personalized content tailored to different audience segments. By analyzing vast amounts of data, AI can generate specific content that resonates with individual preferences. This level of personalization ensures that marketing messages are not only relevant but also engaging for each unique user.

Efficiency

One of the most notable benefits of generative AI is its efficiency. AI can automate content creation, reducing the time and resources needed for manual content generation. This allows marketers to focus on strategic planning and creative ideation.

According to a report by McKinsey, companies using AI for marketing can reduce time spent on repetitive tasks by up to 30%, freeing up valuable resources for more complex activities.

Scalability

Generative AI can handle large volumes of data and interactions simultaneously, making it easier to scale marketing efforts across multiple channels and regions. This scalability ensures consistent messaging and branding, regardless of the audience size or geographic location.

A survey by Salesforce revealed that 51% of marketing leaders already use AI, and 27% plan to incorporate it in the next two years, primarily for its scalability in managing large datasets and broad campaigns.

Data-Driven Decisions

Generative AI continuously analyzes customer data to refine and optimize marketing strategies. This leads to more effective campaigns, as decisions are based on real-time data and insights rather than assumptions.

For example, a study by Deloitte found that companies leveraging AI for data analysis and decision-making experienced a 10% increase in marketing ROI compared to those that did not use AI.

Creative Campaigns

Generative AI has revolutionized the way companies design and implement marketing campaigns. By using advanced algorithms and machine learning, these AI systems can create content, analyze customer interactions, and adjust strategies on the fly, making marketing more dynamic and responsive than ever before.

Real-World Examples of Generative AI in Marketing

- **Wendy's Drive-Thru with Bard AI**: Wendy's implemented a generative AI system named Bard to handle customer orders at the drive-thru. Bard not only takes orders but also offers personalized menu suggestions based on previous orders and popular items. This has increased efficiency and improved the customer experience by understanding and responding to various accents and dialects. This example shows how generative AI can enhance customer interactions while freeing up human employees for other critical tasks.

- **McDonald's and Leo Burnett Thailand**: McDonald's collaborated with Leo Burnett Thailand to use generative AI to create the perfect fried chicken experience. They used ChatGPT to analyze customer preferences and insights about what makes the ideal fried chicken. This AI-driven approach allowed them to innovate quickly and cater specifically to their target market's tastes, showing how AI can speed up product development and marketing processes.

- **Hyperpersonalized Outreach by a European Telecom Company**: A European telecom company utilized generative AI to transition from broad, generic customer outreach to highly personalized messaging. The AI system created tailored communications for 150 specific customer segments, significantly increasing response rates by 40% and reducing deployment costs by 25%. This case illustrates the power of AI in delivering targeted, effective marketing messages that resonate with specific audience segments.

Generative AI has changed how many industries work, especially in marketing. It automates tasks and creates content quickly, but some people worry it might be harming creativity and causing job losses.

Some critics say that while AI can produce a lot of content fast, it often misses the unique creativity that humans bring. For example, AI can generate art and music that copy existing styles, but it might not capture the same emotions or originality that human artists create. In the music world, startups like Suno and Udio have faced legal trouble. Big companies like Sony, Universal, and Warner have sued these AI companies, claiming they used copyrighted music without permission. This legal fight highlights the clash between traditional media companies and new AI technology. The music labels argue that AI-generated content can water down the value of original works, potentially stifling real creativity.

There is also concern about job losses. As AI gets better at doing tasks that humans used to do, there is fear it might replace jobs in various fields. For instance, AI chatbots and customer service tools can handle many customer questions at once, which might reduce the need for human customer service reps. In content creation, AI can write articles, create marketing copy, and even develop scripts, which could impact writers and creative professionals.

A study by the McKinsey Global Institute suggests that automation, including AI, could displace between 400 million and 800 million jobs by 2030. While some jobs will disappear, new ones will be created, especially in AI-related fields. The challenge is making sure workers have the skills to transition to these new roles. In creative industries, there is a special concern about maintaining the human touch in art and expression, which AI might struggle to replicate fully.

The debate about generative AI's impact on creativity and jobs is ongoing. While AI brings efficiency and the ability to scale, it also raises questions about preserving human creativity and the future of work.

Are jobs really being lost, or are we just seeing a shift towards new opportunities in an AI-driven world?

The answer depends on how industries and workers adapt to these technological changes.

Chapter 10
AI's Impact on Marketing Careers

Every time there's a big change in technology, like AI, the way we work changes too. Old jobs might disappear, but new ones come up. This is happening now with AI in marketing.

The skills that marketers need are shifting. It's no longer just about creativity and communication. Now, knowing how to analyze data and use tech tools is just as important. This doesn't mean marketing jobs are disappearing. Instead, new roles like AI specialists and data scientists are becoming part of marketing teams. These new jobs focus on using AI and data to make marketing strategies better.

For those already in marketing, it's important to adapt. Learning new skills and staying updated with the latest technology is crucial. Using AI tools and understanding data can help marketers stay ahead. The future of marketing isn't about fighting against AI, but about growing with it, using it to improve what we do, and finding new ways to succeed.

AI Is Changing Marketing Skills

AI is changing what skills marketers need. It's no longer enough to just be good at creating catchy ads or writing engaging posts. Now, understanding data and using technology are just as important.

Emphasis on Analytics

One of the biggest changes is the need for strong analytical skills. Marketers now need to know how to look at data and understand what it means. This data can come from social media, websites, or customer feedback. By analyzing this data, marketers can learn what customers like and what they don't. This helps them make better decisions about what kind of ads to create and where to show them.

In the past, marketing decisions were often based on intuition or general market trends. Now, with the help of AI, marketers have access to detailed and specific data about customer behavior. For example, social media platforms provide insights into which posts get the most engagement, what times of day people are most active, and which types of content (like videos, images, or articles) are most popular.

Website analytics tools show how visitors interact with a site, where they click, how long they stay on each page, and what leads them to make a purchase. Customer feedback, gathered through surveys or direct interactions, offers valuable insights into what customers think about a product or service, and what improvements they would like to see.

By analyzing this data, marketers can identify patterns and trends. For instance, they might find that a particular age group prefers a certain type of content or that customers are more likely to buy a product after seeing it advertised on a specific platform. With this information, they can tailor their marketing strategies to better meet the needs and preferences of their target audience.

Analytics also helps marketers measure the effectiveness of their campaigns. They can track metrics like click-through rates, conversion rates, and return on investment (ROI) to see which campaigns are working and which are not. This allows them to make data-driven decisions and adjust their strategies in real time, ensuring that their marketing efforts are as effective as possible.

Technical Knowledge

Technical skills are also becoming more important. Marketers need to know how to use AI tools and software. This can include anything from simple tools that help schedule social media posts to complex programs that analyze customer data and predict trends. Understanding these tools can make a marketer's job easier and more effective.

With AI tools, marketers can automate many tasks that used to take a lot of time. For example, scheduling posts on social media can now be done automatically. Tools like Hootsuite and Buffer allow marketers to plan and schedule posts in advance. This not only saves time but also ensures that posts go live at the best times for audience engagement.

For more complex tasks, there are AI programs that can analyze large amounts of data. These programs can look at customer behavior, market trends, and even competitors' activities. By using this data, marketers can predict what products will be popular and what marketing strategies will work best. Tools like Google Analytics and HubSpot provide insights into website traffic and customer interactions, helping marketers refine their strategies.

Understanding how to use these tools effectively is crucial. Marketers need to know how to interpret the data these tools provide and make decisions based on it. This requires a mix of technical skills and analytical thinking. For instance, a marketer might use AI to identify which types of content perform best with their audience and then adjust their content strategy accordingly.

In addition to using AI tools, marketers also need to understand the basics of how these tools work. This includes knowing about algorithms and data processing. While they don't need to be experts in programming, having a basic understanding of how AI processes information can help them use these tools more effectively.

The Blend of Creativity and Technology

While data and technical skills are crucial, creativity is still important. The best marketing strategies combine creative ideas with data-driven insights. For example, a marketer might use data to learn what type of content performs best, and then use their creative skills to make that content interesting and engaging.

Data can tell you what topics your audience cares about, what time they are most active, and which platforms they prefer. However, it's the creative touch that brings this data to life. For instance, if data shows that your audience loves behind-the-scenes content, you can use your creativity to come up with fun and engaging ways to showcase your team and your process.

A creative marketer can take that trend and put a unique spin on it to make it stand out. This could be through a clever social media campaign, an eye-catching video, or an interactive infographic.

Creativity ensures that your content doesn't just blend in with the crowd but grabs attention and encourages interaction.

Balancing creativity with data also helps in developing a brand's voice and identity. Data can help understand what resonates with your audience, but it's creativity that shapes how your brand communicates and connects with people. This blend ensures that your marketing efforts are not only effective but also memorable and relatable.

Continuous Learning

The field of AI and marketing is always changing. New tools and technologies are constantly being developed. This means that marketers need to keep learning new skills throughout their careers. Taking online courses, attending workshops, and staying up-to-date with industry news are all ways to keep skills sharp.

To stay relevant, marketers need to be proactive about learning. This might involve enrolling in online courses that cover the latest in AI and data analytics or attending industry conferences where experts share new insights and technologies. Subscribing to industry newsletters and following thought leaders on social media can also help marketers stay informed about the latest trends and best practices.

Continuous learning helps marketers understand new tools and how to use them effectively. For example, learning about a new AI tool that can predict customer behavior can give a marketer a significant edge. By understanding how to implement this tool, they can better anticipate customer needs and tailor their marketing strategies accordingly.

Collaboration

With these changes, collaboration has also become more important. Marketers need to work closely with data analysts and IT professionals. Understanding how to communicate and collaborate with these experts can help create more effective marketing strategies.

In the modern marketing landscape, a single person rarely possesses all the skills needed to execute a comprehensive marketing strategy. Marketers often need to collaborate with data analysts who can provide insights into customer behavior and market trends. These analysts use data to identify patterns and predict outcomes, which marketers can then use to shape their campaigns.

Collaboration with IT professionals is also crucial. As AI tools and technologies become more integrated into marketing strategies, understanding how to implement and maintain these tools is essential. IT professionals can help set up and manage AI tools, ensuring they function correctly and provide accurate data.

Effective communication is key in these collaborations. Marketers need to clearly articulate their goals and strategies so that data analysts and IT professionals understand what is needed. This collaboration ensures that everyone is working towards the same objectives, making marketing efforts more cohesive and efficient.

AI Specialists and Data Scientists in Marketing

As AI becomes more integrated into marketing, new job roles are emerging to meet the demand for specialized skills. Two key roles that have gained prominence are AI specialists and data scientists within marketing departments.

AI Specialists

AI specialists are experts in developing and implementing AI technologies. In a marketing context, their job is to design and manage AI systems that can enhance marketing strategies. These specialists have a deep understanding of machine learning algorithms, natural language processing, and other AI technologies. Their expertise allows them to create tools that can analyze customer data, predict trends, and automate various marketing tasks.

For instance, AI specialists might develop chatbots that can interact with customers in real time, answering questions and providing personalized recommendations. They can also create systems that analyze social media trends to help marketers stay ahead of the competition. By leveraging AI, these specialists help make marketing more efficient and effective.

Data Scientists

Data scientists play a crucial role in interpreting the vast amounts of data generated by AI tools. Their job is to analyze this data and extract valuable insights that can inform marketing strategies. Data scientists are skilled in statistical analysis, data mining, and programming languages like Python and R.

In a marketing department, data scientists might look at customer behavior patterns to determine what types of products are most popular or which marketing campaigns are most effective. They can also use predictive analytics to forecast future trends, helping companies to plan their strategies accordingly. By turning raw data into actionable insights, data scientists ensure that marketing decisions are data-driven and targeted.

Prompt Engineers

Prompt engineers are emerging as a new and crucial role in the world of AI-driven marketing. These professionals specialize in creating and refining prompts that guide AI systems to produce the desired content or responses. Their work involves understanding the nuances of language and how AI interprets it to ensure that the AI outputs are relevant and effective.

In marketing, prompt engineers might develop specific prompts that help AI generate engaging social media posts, compelling ad copy, or personalized email content. Their expertise ensures that the AI understands the brand's voice and objectives, leading to more accurate and impactful content creation.

The Integration of These Roles

The integration of AI specialists, data scientists, and prompt engineers into marketing teams represents a significant shift in how marketing is conducted. These roles work closely with traditional marketing professionals to create a more data-driven marketing approach. This collaboration ensures that marketing strategies are not only creative but also backed by solid data and cutting-edge technology.

For example, a marketing team planning a new campaign might work with AI specialists to develop a tool that predicts customer responses to different types of content. Data scientists can then analyze the results to determine which content performs best. Prompt engineers can fine-tune the AI prompts to ensure the generated content aligns perfectly with the campaign's goals. This data-driven approach allows marketers to refine their strategies in real-time, making them more effective and responsive to customer needs.

AI specialists focus on building and managing AI systems. They ensure these systems are efficient and effective in gathering and processing data. Data scientists then take this processed data and analyze it to find patterns and insights. These insights help in understanding customer behavior and preferences. Prompt engineers work to make sure that the AI-generated content is accurate and aligns with the marketing goals.

This collaboration helps marketing teams create personalized and engaging content. For instance, if the data shows that a certain type of content gets more engagement, the team can quickly adapt and produce more of that content. This way, marketing strategies become more flexible and responsive to customer feedback.

Adapting to Change

Adapting to change is always important, especially with AI transforming marketing jobs.

First, keep learning. The world of AI and marketing is always changing. Take online courses, attend workshops, and read the latest industry news to stay up-to-date, and get comfortable with AI tools. These might help you analyze customer data or create content. The more you know about these tools, the better you can use them.

Understanding data is key. Learn how to read and use data to make decisions. This will help you improve your marketing strategies with real information. Working with others is also important. Team up with AI specialists and data scientists to learn how to use AI tools effectively. This teamwork will help you create better marketing strategies. Creativity still matters. Think of new and interesting ways to engage your audience. Use AI to gather information and let your creativity shine through.

Be flexible. The marketing world is always changing, and being open to learning new skills and trying new tools will help you stay ahead, and build your network. Connect with other marketing professionals. Attend industry events, join online forums, and participate in discussions. Networking can provide valuable insights and opportunities.

As AI keeps advancing, everything, including marketing careers, will change. This brings both new opportunities and challenges. By staying flexible, learning new skills, and working with technology, you can succeed in this exciting field.

The future of marketing is full of possibilities. Stay open to change, keep growing, and be ready for the new opportunities ahead. The path may be different, but it's full of potential and excitement.

Chapter 11
The Future of AI in Marketing

Businesses are going to evolve. A few years ago, none of us even knew that social media could become so important for making money. Back then, it was just a place to connect with friends, share pictures, and follow pages you liked. But now, it has turned into a big tool for businesses to reach people, advertise their products, and even start new brands. The way we see marketing has changed a lot, and it's not just happening online. Marketing has become a part of almost everything we do.

Think about it. Every time you scroll through Instagram, Facebook, or YouTube, you're being shown ads, and often you don't even notice it. These ads are made just for you, based on what you've liked, watched, or searched for. From the food you order to the shoes you buy, everything is influenced by how marketing has grown. It's not just the businesses that are changing; we are, too. We're always interacting with these types of marketing, sometimes without even realizing it. It's become a normal part of our daily lives.

But it's not only social media. When you walk through a city, you see marketing everywhere. Billboards, buses, and even park benches have ads on them. When you watch a show on streaming services, they recommend things based on what you've watched before. Apps on your phone track what you do and suggest things you might like. The world around us is filled with marketing in ways we don't always notice. This is not a new thing—marketing has always been there. What started as simple word-of-mouth or newspaper ads has now become about algorithms, influencers, and using data to create targeted ads.

So, what will the future of marketing be? Can AI be the solution?

AI has opened up a lot of possibilities for marketing. It can help businesses make smarter decisions, reach people in new ways, and even personalize how they interact with customers. There's no doubt that AI can make marketing more efficient and beneficial. But, like with any new tool or technology, the key is how we choose to use it.

The future of marketing with AI can be amazing, but it's important to remember that AI is just a tool. It's not going to replace everything, and it's not going to make all decisions for us. Human beings are still at the heart of it all. We have to guide AI, decide how to use the information it gives us, and most importantly, keep the human touch alive in the way we connect with others. AI can help us do better, but it's up to us to use it wisely.

But what about marketing? This is one area where AI's impact will be especially significant. Imagine receiving offers and advertisements that seem to read your mind—suggestions that are exactly what you're looking for, just when you need them. Companies will use AI to deeply understand customer behavior, allowing them to create marketing campaigns that are more effective and personalized.

The future could be more exciting and unpredictable than we can imagine. We might see flying taxis zipping through the skies, and homes that adjust the temperature, lighting, and even the music to fit our moods without us lifting a finger. Everyday tasks like shopping or managing our finances could become incredibly easy, thanks to smart systems that understand our preferences better than we do.

In this ever-changing world, AI is set to play a central role. It won't just be a tool; it could become a true partner in our daily lives. Think of it: you're walking down the street, and your AI assistant finds the perfect place for lunch and suggests a new pair of shoes based on what you've recently browsed online. At work, AI could help you sift through mountains of data, predict trends, and even draft content, freeing you up to focus on bigger, creative ideas.

In the end, the future with AI is full of possibilities. But it's up to us to make sure, possibilities are used to build a better world, where technology serves us, supports our goals, and helps us live better lives.

How important is it to stay updated with AI advancements and build a culture of innovation and learning?

As we look ahead, one thing becomes very clear—AI is moving fast. It's changing the way businesses run and the way we do marketing. To keep up, it's important to stay updated with the advancements in AI. New tools and methods are constantly coming out, and if we're not paying attention, we might miss out on opportunities that could help us grow.

Keeping up with AI isn't just about understanding the latest trends, though. It's about creating an environment where learning and innovation are always encouraged. No matter how advanced AI gets, the human element will always matter. People still need to ask the right questions, think creatively, and find new ways to solve problems. AI can help us, but it's our mindset that will truly push things forward.

When you build a culture of learning, you're not just reacting to changes—you're preparing for them. You're thinking ahead and staying open to new ideas. Whether you're a business owner, a marketer, or just someone interested in how AI can improve things, it's important to keep learning, experimenting, and trying out new approaches. That's how real progress happens.

AI in marketing holds a lot of promise, but that promise is only realized when we combine it with a mindset of curiosity and growth. It's easy to get caught up in the excitement of new technology, but the real key to success is to always keep learning and to be open to new possibilities.

It's not just about using AI—it's about how we use it.

Is AI in Marketing: A Personalized Experience?

When you scroll through apps or shop online, the ads or product suggestions you see often seem like they know exactly what you're looking for. That's because AI is working behind the scenes to make it happen. It uses information about your past searches, clicks, and purchases to show you products that match your preferences.

AI in marketing is focused on personalization. It collects data based on what you do—what you browse, what you like, and what you buy. Using this, businesses can offer you things that are more relevant to you, making your experience smoother and more tailored.

Personalization through AI isn't limited to just ads. When you visit a website, AI might change the products or services displayed, based on what you've shown interest in before. If you've bought a certain product, it may suggest items that go well with it. If you're a first-time visitor, it might show you what's popular. This makes your time on the site more convenient and helpful.

The real strength of AI is that it works in the background. It learns from your behavior without you having to tell it what you like. It's like having someone in the store who remembers you every time you visit, always ready to recommend something based on your tastes.

While AI can make marketing more personal, it's important to remember that it's a tool. It's there to make things easier and more relevant, but it needs to be used wisely. The aim is to create a better experience, not to bombard you with too much information.

Is This The Conclusion?

AI in marketing is just beginning. AI has already made big changes, helping businesses reach people in smarter, faster, and more personalized ways. But there's so much more ahead. AI will continue to improve, but how it shapes the future will depend on how we decide to use it.

AI has the potential to make marketing more efficient and customer-focused, but it's still a tool. It needs thoughtful use and human guidance. The magic of AI lies in its ability to assist us, not replace us. The human element—our creativity, and our understanding of people—will always matter. AI can help businesses offer better experiences, but it's up to us to decide what that future looks like.

As AI continues to evolve, we'll see more changes, but one thing remains certain: marketing will continue to grow and adapt with us, finding new ways to fit into our everyday lives.

This is the last page of this book, but it leaves us with one question: *if AI is transforming marketing so quickly, what will its impact be on other industries?* **The possibilities are limitless.**

Author Bio

Tamil Selvi K Ganesan holds a Master of Business Administration with a major in marketing from Universiti Teknologi Malaysia. She further expanded her expertise by completing a Professional Master's Degree in Artificial Intelligence, specializing in Marketing and Communication, from Tech Global University in 2024. Her academic journey shows a strong dedication to learning and growth.

She is deeply passionate about the future of AI and its role in shaping the world of marketing. This journey would not have been possible without her family's support, and she is incredibly grateful for their encouragement every step of the way. She thanks everyone for being a part of this exciting journey with her!